JESUS TIME

Love Notes of Wonder and Worship

Judith Rolfs

Dedicated to:

All People Everywhere

Beloved By Jesus

Copyright 2018

Publishers Wayne and Judith Rolfs
Wisconsin, USA

Dear Reader,

I hope these love notes will excite and thrill your heart. Jesus is truly the lover you've longed for and the power that energizes your life.

My life has not always been easy or fair. I began my spiritual search as a disbeliever, studied the ideas of many faiths and examined their impact upon people's lives.

Over the years, I've seen Jesus act on my behalf in miraculous ways, whether I was facing blindness, liver failure or the near death of a child. Throughout life's ups and downs I've come to know how amazing Jesus is. If you let Him, Jesus will impact your world too.

Jesus Time, Love Notes of Wonder and Worship, messages have come to me in middle of the night awakenings, morning moments before Him and at unexpected times throughout the day. Jesus is always present. We need only listen and speak to Him. Why not start a prayer journal and keep it beside you as you read.

May these meditations resonate with you. My prayer is that they'll make spiritual sense in your soul and you'll be as breathlessly in love with Jesus, as He is with you.

Judith Rolfs

Your Presence

Dear Jesus,

I love to think of You as my fiery God not contained in anything physical. You bring life to souls, nations and worlds. You're the movement within every moment and the thought source behind all meaning.

There's nowhere I'd rather be today, tomorrow or for eternity than in Your Presence and at the very center Your will.

You make my soul glow and fill me with peace. I searched for You and You found me. My spirit shouts with joy. Does all the universe hear?

Isaiah 49:16
See, I have inscribed you on the palms of My hands; Your walls are continually before Me.

January 2

Faith

Dear Jesus,

With the tiniest of breaths, I call to You and speak words of praise. There's always something to be grateful for. You're continually worthy of an alleluia. The chorus of nature joins me in celebrating You daily. Sky, earth, air clap in unison and my faith is strengthened. The God of the past is the God of now. The God of tomorrow is forever trustworthy and merciful.

Even today, as troubles surround me, my knees bend in worship. My pleasant normality is gone. The problems in my life leave me gasping. My trials are here, but my soul takes up heavenly residence with You in words of praise.

This is faith, the power that trusts in Your deliverance, stops my fears and restores my peace.

Revelation 21:3-4
And I heard a loud voice from the throne saying, "Look! God's dwelling place is now among the people, and He will dwell with them. They will be His people, and God Himself will be with them and be their God. He will wipe every tear from their eyes."

January 3

Maker of Earth

Dear Jesus,

Creator of Light, Maker of this amazing earth, without Your design our majestic world wouldn't exist. How exciting it must have been when You finished and looked at the world You made. You'd never created a world before! What an excellent masterpiece of land and seas You designed.

You gave authority over earth to human heads and hands. Dangerous power, perhaps? Would You trust us if You had it to do over again? I believe you'd say yes, because human freedom is important to You.

Jesus, may I make wise choices in protecting Your world. What a privilege to use my gifts to make a personal impact on Your wondrous world.

Col 1:16-17
For in Him all things in heaven and on earth were created, things visible and invisible, whether thrones or dominions or rulers or powers—all things have been created through Him and for Him. He himself is before all things, and in Him all things hold together.

January 4

Valuable Leisure

Dear Jesus,

How I need Your Holy Spirit's wisdom and discernment! I realize my best plans come after seeking Your direction. All that's done of real significance centers on You and flows through You.

Why do I sometimes let my days become crazy, chaotic, charged by must-do's and excessive self-focus? Way too often I block simple, joy-filled, peaceful living. Help me avoid the useless activities I can easily drift into. Real leisure is valuable.

I must be ruthlessly unbusy at times during my day to hear You. Then I can flow with Your purposes in all my work and play. I need to refresh myself often, Jesus, as You did by time with our Father. Only then will my work and leisure glorify You in every way.

Exodus 33:14
The Lord replied, "My Presence will go with you, and I will give you rest."

January 5

Special Places

Dear Jesus,

There are special places I'd like to have been with You when You walked earth. How exciting to have stood alongside You at the edge of the lake and watch Peter scurry toward You across the water. I'd love to see Your hands flip fish over a fire at the shore breakfast You cooked for Your disciples. What fun to observe Your interactions with guests at the wedding feast as you all enjoyed the celebration!

What a thrill to have been present to hear You read Isaiah in the temple and proclaim before Your listeners: "Today, these words have been fulfilled in your presence!" Was the shock, the silence, deafening?

Jesus, even as I imagine these scenes from the past, I treasure Your invisible Presence in my life today! I savor each special place of connection I've experienced with You.

John 3:30
He [Jesus] must become greater; I must become less.

January 6

Nature's Beauty

Dear Jesus,

Absolutely nothing surpasses the beauty You created in nature! You bless me with sunsets that dazzle my vision and defy verbal description. I'm enthralled with Your lavish designs of exquisite snowflakes and intricate cell structures. I'm amazed at the variety in human eyes and noses and mouths. The range of colors in Your incredible array of flowers and the sky overhead enthralls me every day.

I marvel at Your strong aesthetic sense. I delight in lovely settings too. Beautiful things made by human minds and hands are also impressive.

The clothing I wear pales next to nature's gorgeous colors and designs. My house is comfortable but not perfectly decorated. Yet Your world always is lovely Jesus. You generously display Your beauty everywhere - I need only look. All about me I sense Your magnificence.

Psalm 27:4
One thing I ask from the Lord, this only do I seek: that I may dwell in the house of the Lord all the days of my life, to gaze on the beauty the Lord and to seek Him in His temple.

January 7

"Tude"

Dear Jesus,

What "tude" shall mine be? What atti-tude will I show? Will it be excitement for every new day of life? A sense of wondrous expectation regarding everyone I meet? Will I find delight in my circumstances whatever? Or will I be a grumbler and complain that life is a monotonous, dreary routine filled with boring people? The choice is mine.

Shall I be self-centered or God-focused? Lord, it's up to me to decide my "tude" which is hugely important. "Tude" determines if my days are savored or dreaded, enjoyed or endured.

The choice is clear. The "tude" pleasing to You, Lord, is one of grati-tude. Every day I choose the "tude" of trust and delight myself in You, Lord.

Psalm 16:8-9
I keep my eyes always on the Lord. With Him at my right hand, I will not be shaken. Therefore my heart is glad and my tongue rejoices; my body also will rest secure.

Scripture's Feast

Dear Jesus,

I savor all the nourishment within Your Word. I feast on it to stay well fed. Psalms, Proverbs, stories of Biblical heroes, sinners' warnings, and great promises of good yet-to-come teach and inspire me.

The Our Father prayer reminds me I'm privileged to receive daily bread from Your hand. You feed me physically and spiritually. I can ask to be delivered from evil and live without fear.

Through Scripture You give me wisdom and courage to do Your will. How I treasure each truth. The health of my body, soul and spirit is sustained through this sumptuous feast.

Luke 24:45
Then He opened their minds so they could understand the Scriptures.

January 9

Amazing

Dear Jesus,

You're the destroyer of darkness and the glow within every vision of beauty. I know You're the source of all meaning, the sensation behind all love, and the force inspiring every act of charity. Oh Creator, You exceed my comprehension.

Amazing Saint-Maker, Powerful Sin-Eliminator, Eternal Beloved Lord and God! How thrilling it is to know and love You. What a privilege to serve You and Your people!

You truly are the one, living God.

Psalm 63:1-8
You, God, are my God, earnestly I seek you; I thirst for You, my whole being longs for You, in a dry and parched land where there is no water. I have seen You in the sanctuary and beheld Your power and Your glory. Because Your love is better than life, my lips will glorify You.

Quiet Christian

Dear Jesus,

I've been too quiet a Christian at times. I haven't always spoken out about You with total boldness. No death plots have been planned for me like those designed for Paul. I haven't risked prison or suffered hardships for my faith.

I've rarely, if ever, been made the brunt of laughter or ostracized from the company of others for my faith. When was I last ridiculed for speaking about You?

Jesus, may I become braver like Paul, who said, "I've never hesitated to preach, proclaiming the whole will of God." Help me speak Your truth to every individual I encounter. May I remember how You shocked listeners with Your words of life. You submitted to a horrid death for the good that would come to others! Empower me to be a bolder Christian.

Ephesians 3: 7-9
I became a servant of this gospel by the gift of God's grace given me through the working of His power. Although I am less than the least of all the Lord's people, this grace was given me: to preach to the Gentiles the boundless riches of Christ...

January 11

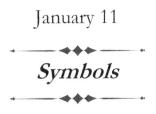

Symbols

Dear Jesus,

You often used symbols to tell listeners about Yourself. I like to ponder each of them. You're like a gate to walk through, a door to open and bread to taste and be nourished by. You're like water that sustains life and a shepherd who guides and protects.

These simple images are meaningful concrete symbols of who You are. They signify You're real and present in power for me.

I become easily distracted by the world around me with its continual allure. How quickly I forget my divine purpose and Your provision in my life. I treasure these simple symbolic reminders.

Psalm 23
The Lord is my shepherd, I lack nothing. He makes me lie down in green pastures. He leads me beside quiet waters. He refreshes my soul. He guides me along the right paths for His name's sake. Even though I walk through the darkest valley, I will fear no evil, for You are with me; Your rod and Your staff they comfort me. You prepare a table before me in the presence of my enemies. You anoint my head with oil; my cup overflows.

January 12

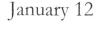

Possibilities

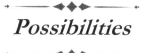

Dear Jesus,

I've had unfulfilled longings and walked the edge of despair. Life hasn't always been easy. Sometimes I've succumbed to Satan through my wrong desires and actions. At times I realize I've sought personal glory while persuading myself I was promoting You. Often my efforts have been misdirected.

Snatch me out of these dark places and foolishness. Lift me from Satan's clutches. Renew my youthful energy and bless me in the sight of my enemies. Nurture me with Your tenderness.

I confess my failures and misdirected motives. Jesus, what I once thought important isn't. Your truth in Scripture reminds me Your way is always best. I delight now and forever in exalting You. Every day is rich with possibilities for Your glory. You bring me my deepest joy.

Psalm 96:1-6
Sing to the Lord a new song; sing to the Lord, all the earth. Sing to the Lord, praise His name; proclaim His salvation day after day. Declare His glory among the nations, His marvelous deeds among all peoples. For great is the Lord and most worthy of praise.

January 13

Mountain-moving

Dear Jesus,

You've taught me to speak to an obstacle like a mountain with faith and it will move. Often I must first move the mountain within me - my human inertia, my tendency to doubt, and my self-absorption. These massively impede my efforts. Simple pure laziness can block action for Your kingdom. How sad. This must displease You immensely.

When I exercise my faith it becomes stronger. "Mountain move out of the way. I intend to remove every obstacle and take steps to bear fruit as my Master directs."

Jesus, faith in You is the power source that accomplishes all things and works all things for good - beginnings and endings. You truly are the Alpha and Omega Jesus, my all in all.

Matthew 17:20
He [Jesus] replied, "Because you have so little faith. Truly I tell you, if you have faith as small as a mustard seed, you can say to this mountain, 'Move from here to there,' and it will move. Nothing will be impossible for you."

January 14

Controversy

Dear Jesus,

What controversy You stirred! People disputed that You were a good man. Many thought You deceived and misled the masses. The mystery of Your past baffled the Pharisees. Where had You acquired such extensive knowledge of Scripture? You'd never studied with a rabbi.

You shocked listeners when You proclaimed that all people could know God the Father through You. Many were confused. No one had expected a gentle, humble Messiah.

You emerged from Bethlehem and Nazareth. You said You hadn't come of Your own accord, but God the Father sent you! How shocking. I like to imagine the uproar around You and the excitement in the hearts of those who finally believed. I know the thrill in my heart when I did!

John 7:12-18

Not until halfway through the festival did Jesus go up to the temple courts and begin to teach. The Jews there were amazed and asked, "How did this man get such learning without having been taught?" Jesus answered, "My teaching is not My own. It comes from the One who sent Me. Anyone who chooses to do the will of God will find out whether My teaching comes from God or whether I speak on My own."

January 15

Spirit Check Over

Dear Jesus,

A Spirit check-over is needed. Please remove my sore spots from hurtful treatment I've received and from words that wounded me. Soften my tendency to respond with harshness, Jesus. How about a soul examination, a spirit check over, a goodness-shine, and a heart touch - the works if You please.

Remove a critical spirit from me. I mustn't find fault with others over petty differences. Pettiness is unbecoming a Spirit-filled believer.

Words have power and can easily fragment relationships. May my mouth speak with kindness even to those who have mouths like swords. Spirit of God, may I filter every word through You to uplift others. I long to reflect the loving heart and sweet spirit pleasing to You. Check me over often, Jesus.

I Corinthians 13 1-5
If I speak in the tongues of men or of angels, but do not have love, I am only a resounding gong or a clanging cymbal. If I have the gift of prophecy and can fathom all mysteries and all knowledge, and if I have a faith that can move mountains, but do not have love, I am nothing.

January 16

Final Nights

Dear Jesus,

I've been at the bedside of people during their final hours on earth. I know fear can grip hard on deathbeds before that momentous journey into eternity. It's difficult for those who only played with belief during the evaporating hours of life. Jesus, pour faith like strong rain into trembling souls such as these. Keep them from the devil's discouragement that leads to despair.

Replace their dance of doubt and fright with total faith, Jesus. A little glimpse of glory may be all they need. Precious Jesus, help them enter eternity with a triumphant breath of trust.

I've also been with individuals who are minutes from death but are seeped in peace and breathe deep, contented breaths. They expectantly and excitedly await seeing You Lord. When the time arrives for my final life's journey may my faith be steadfast.

Matthew 4:16
The people living in darkness have seen a great light; on those living in the land of the shadow of death a light has dawned.

January 17

A Few Questions

Dear Jesus,

I've a few questions for You. Do You play in heaven? How? Is that what happens when the trees dance in the wind and the rain turns off and on? Is making sunbeams streak a game for you? Does birthing ideas in men's brains excite You? Do You like seeing hybrids created from Your species? Does my laughter make You laugh?

What does it feel like to guide a universe? How do you deal with Your sadness when we go astray? What's it like to watch murderers rage, to allow natural calamities that kill? I'm sure it's hard. But You also see the joy in heaven when the angels rejoice at the entrance of new souls.

How do You work all things for good in human beings who place their trust in You? Is it difficult to do this for all of us? I marvel at Your amazing ways! I can't wait to ask You these questions face to face.

Galatians 4:16-18
My counsel is this: Live freely, animated and motivated by God's Spirit.

January 18

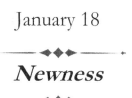

Newness

Dear Jesus,

The world is always new because of You, brightened and redesigned with daily regularity. Each twenty-four hours tells a story of Your sustaining care. Days unfold one by one initiated and completed according to Your plan.

I marvel at earth's changing seasons. I want to shout "See Jesus' creativity!" I stand at the foot of mighty mountains and yell "See Your strength." I look at fields ripe with crops and shout: "See Your provision."

Jesus, because of You, all this exists. All that needs to be will be, all that is can become good. With the hosts of heaven I praise You Lord for Your works of newness and sameness as well.

Psalm 145:10
All Your works praise you, Lord; Your faithful people extol you.

January 19

Wealth

Dear Jesus,

Your generosity to me enables me to manage my own needs plus help others.

Still I often require reminders and nudges to give financial help. It can be tempting to ignore the needs of others. I know holding money too dearly can originate from fear, a history of lack, or hoarding - the sin of selfishness. I'm ashamed how often I've neglected generosity for the poor while clinging to my fickle, fleeting finances.

Wealth can be an emotional and spiritual block. Jesus, true riches are found in faithful obedience to Your will. It's not hard to give ten per cent from my surplus energy and money but I need to do much more. Help me give to the point of self-denial with cheer and extravagant generosity.

Psalm 49:10-13
For all can see that the wise die, that the foolish and the senseless also perish, leaving their wealth to others. Their tombs will remain their houses forever, their dwellings for endless generations, though they had named lands after themselves. People, despite their wealth, do not endure; they are like the beasts that perish.

January 20

Untangled

Dear Jesus,

In the morning I examine my lists of to-dos. They're like swirly strands within my mind entangling me. Too much to do, too little time.

Holy Spirit, help me deal with each item one by one. Let me not be trapped in unproductivity, or over focused on small accomplishments to the neglect of your grandest plan. Untangle me please. Help me live this day radiantly and grace-filled.

I pause to pray and sense Your supernatural power freeing me from stress. Your grace is so thick I inhale it. You uplift me physically and spiritually. I'm at peace, ready to venture forth into my day.

Isaiah 26:3
You will keep in perfect peace those whose minds are steadfast, because they trust in You.

January 21

Revelation

Dear Jesus,

The numbers in Revelation signify what comes in the future. One throne in heaven encircled by an emerald rainbow. Four living creatures, a lion, ox, man and flying eagle surround it. Six wings on each creature are covered with eyes all around.

Seven lamps blaze before the throne, 24 elders in white with golden crowns, 24 golden bowls filled with the saints' prayers, and 24 thrones for them to sit. 10,000 x 10,000 angels around the throne, one scroll is sealed with seven seals. One incomparable Lion of Judah opens the scroll! What a scene.

The sounds of heaven are equally amazing. Countless rumblings and peals of thunder with numerous flashes of lightning will strike awe in observers. One day, all mankind shall bow, and every heart will show honor to You in this huge scene of praise!

Revelation 4:1
After this I looked, and there before me was a door standing open in heaven. And the voice I had first heard speaking to me like a trumpet said, "Come up here, and I will show you what must take place after this."

January 22

Heaven's Pages

Dear Jesus,

How amazing that ever-watchful angels joyfully record each new life's spiritual progress on heaven's pages when empty souls and needy bodies discover You - the One who alone can fill every need. Gratefully, my name is written there.

Your Spirit inspires my godly human actions as I go about the days of my life protected by angelic guardians. Divinity resides within me when I demonstrate Our Father's love and perform His will upon earth.

I'm eager to meet angels face-to-face one day and read the Book of Life. Meanwhile I hope to help add a few names. May these pages multiply beyond measure.

Luke 15:10
In the same way, I tell you, there is rejoicing in the presence of the angels of God over one sinner who repents.

January 23

"ITY"

Dear Jesus,

You've made me a lover of words and languages. I especially like those that end it "ity." Living honorably in real-ity requires integr-ity, which also requires sincer-ity and frequently leads to prosper-ity, best enjoyed with matur-ity.

All these are hallmarks of Christian-ity. With all my heart, I seek these ITY's.

Yet these are nothing compared to one thing of ultimate value. Jesus, may my soul thrive in etern-ity with You.

Proverbs 26:1-4
Like snow in summer or rain in harvest, honor is not fitting for a fool. Like a fluttering sparrow or a darting swallow, an undeserved curse does not come to rest. A whip for the horse, a bridle for the donkey, and a rod for the backs of fools! Do not answer a fool according to his folly, or you yourself will be just like him.

January 24

Loving Well

Dear Jesus,

Please excuse my snaps of judgment when I've climbed on my imaginary throne of self-righteousness. Sanctify any wrong attitude from a faulty sense of superiority. Help me love others as You do.

Judging souls of non-Christians has no place in a life of holiness. Judgment reeks of personal pride and deprives others of respect. It excludes gentle mercy and alienates others. Judgment blocks my compassion. Yet, it's right to judge the actions of Christians who violate Your commandments. I must always speak out against gross evil and injustice.

I can encourage me fellow Christians to stop sinning by asking kind questions, making thoughtful suggestions, and humbly teaching. These powerful acts of blessing transform people in ways that judging could never do.

Matthew 7:1-4
Do not judge, or you too will be judged. For in the same way you judge others, you will be judged, and with the measure you use, it will be measured to you.

January 25

Good News Bearers

Dear Jesus,

I hear Christians say they're soul winning as if a soul is a trophy. Or sinner-saving as if that's humanly possible when it's truly a work of Your Holy Spirit. Salvation is sometimes thought of as a "help-a-person say-the-right –words-to-be-saved" event.

Instead, we're each simply to be a "good news bearer". This old-fashioned biblical phrase fits well. My job is to describe Your amazing acts and speak Your words of truth. Then Your sweet gift of grace flows and prompts souls to experience spirit-life. This good news truly has power to redeem.

I simply tell what I know about You and give listeners a choice to accept or reject You. All responsibility for belief and transformation resides in the receiver. Joy and peace throughout eternity are the sweet rewards for those who choose You. Thanks for making this clear and keeping it uncomplicated.

Luke 2:10
But the angel said to them, "Do not be afraid. I bring you good news that will cause great joy for all the people.

January 26

Riddles

Dear Jesus,

You often spoke in riddles and gave strange commands to people like telling a man to dip in the lake seven times. The methods You used made people think deeply and respond humbly. It also made observers wonder.

Jesus, You equip me with the ability to unravel puzzles and decipher truth. I acquire knowledge as I study facts in Your Word and sincerely search for understanding. I like Your riddles.

I probe Your communication methods Jesus and study the consequences of following Your way. Riddles unravel into solid logic. Your commands stem from incredible love. Riddles and mysteries display Your incomparable wisdom.

Ephesians 3:3-5
...that is, the mystery made known to me by revelation, as I [Paul] have already written briefly. In reading this, then, you will be able to understand my insight into the mystery of Christ, which was not made known to people in other generations as it has now been revealed by the Spirit to God's holy apostles and prophets.

January 27

Simply Giving

Dear Jesus,

Your Word teaches clearly that giving is important in Your sight. Though my resources are limited, You encourage my generosity. May I not neglect anyone who needs a financial blessing when it's in my power to give.

I used to think giving was about helping others - blessing the poor with my gifts. This is true, of course, but Your word teaches that blessings also come to me from my giving. I never knew I could receive such great delight from giving and seeing the joy I'm able to bring to others.

I've been bountifully blessed. Jesus, may I be a bountiful blesser as well, like You.

Acts 10:31
An angel of the Lord in dazzling apparel said, "Cornelius, your donations to the poor have been known and preserved before God. God heeds and is about to help you."

January 28

The Grand Pretend

Dear Jesus,

Having and doing, moving and grooving. Life on the surface can be a grand pretend. Smiles and laughter conceal emptiness. How well I know. I performed this dance until the day the questions became too strong and I had to know: Is this all there is? Shouldn't there be more meaning in this splendid drama of life?

Somehow hearts know there is more to living than chasing about. Someone, somewhere must have answers. How about the One who made the universe itself?

Jesus, You showed me life beyond the surface and taught me what real living is. The essence of joy is abandoning self-focus and, wonder of wonders, serving others. No pretense works, only simple, authentic wholeness and purposeful living according to Your exquisite plan for life.

Romans 6:5-6
For if we have been united with Him in a death like His, we will certainly also be united with Him in a resurrection like His. For we know that our old self was crucified with Him so that the body ruled by sin might be done away with, that we should no longer be slaves to sin.

January 29

Sacrifice of Praise

Dear Jesus,

I wonder…how can worship be a sacrifice when praising You is such a joy? I recall the sacrifice of praise made by Job when all he possessed was destroyed and nothing he treasured remained. Yet even then Job said and meant with all his heart: "Blessed be the name of the Jesus, the Lord gives and takes away, blessed be His name!"

The sacrifice of praise is soul food. It keeps me spiritually nourished and joyful. Through it, I acknowledge You're my Faithful King and Restorer. I have a Creator and a Better-Maker. Jesus, You make all things new – yes all things do work for good! You're a good-from-evil Designer.

The power within the sacrifice of praise is incomprehensible to me –but effective and true. How I thank You!

Job 1:20-22
At this, Job got up and tore his robe and shaved his head. Then he fell to the ground in worship and said "Naked I came from my mother's womb and naked I will depart. The Lord gave and the Lord has taken away; may the name of the Lord be praised." In all this, Job did not sin by charging God with wrongdoing.

January 30

Seasons

Dear Jesus,

You've set the seasons for my life. You know how many there will be. In winter's cold I find warmth. You plan for my growth in December's darkness, and inspire me to flower. In autumn's death, I become renewed. In June's brightness, I feel delicious joy, in spring your pruning is tender.

I am not dependent on weather's frivolity. Any season becomes one of beauty as You nurture and transfigure nature and me.

Each season has been pre-ordained by You. My responsibility and privilege is to make each one significant through maximizing everyday life with You.

Ecclesiastes 3:1-8
There is a time for everything, and a season for every activity under the heavens: a time to be born and a time to die, a time to plant and a time to uproot, a time to kill and a time to heal, a time to tear down and a time to build, a time to weep and a time to laugh, a time to mourn and a time to dance, a time to scatter stones and a time to gather them, … a time to keep and a time to throw away, a time to tear and a time to mend, a time to be silent and a time to speak, a time to love and a time to hate, a time for war and a time for peace.

January 31

―――◆◆◆―――

Hear Me

―――◆◆◆―――

Dear Jesus,

In my heart I hear You saying: "Hear Me! I am Christ of the Catholics, I am Christ of the Lutherans, I am Christ of the Methodists, I am Christ of the Pentecostals, I am Christ of all Christian denominations, I am Christ the originator of all."

"You people are my church. My message of salvation is universal. Look to me, not to ritual or selective truths. My good news is simple. Stop making it complex. Open the gates for all, remove the barriers."

"Stand in unity with the Father, Son and Holy Spirit. My church is one! My church is holy! Stop destroying brothers and sisters. Uphold one another, my children. You are one in Me. Build my body on earth. Judge not. Treasure one another with love. Respect and celebrate your differences even as you embrace unity. Make my earthly body strong." Jesus, I promise I will do my part.

John 17:20
[The words of Jesus] "My prayer is not for them alone. I pray also for those who will believe in me through their message..."

February 1

Foretaste

Dear Jesus,

You're like solar power streaming into me. Your energy pervades all my moments. Every day I celebrate living life with You. You shower me with gifts of grace and strength continually.

You bring me moments of intense rapture and clarity of purpose. This must be what's meant by foretaste divine.

You play a gargantuan role in each person's world. How amazing that You generously offer Your presence to everyone dear Jesus. No wonder the Psalmist sings of Your great love forever. So shall I!

Psalm 89:1-2
I will sing of the Lord's great love forever; with my mouth I will make Your faithfulness known through all generations. I will declare that Your love stands firm forever, that You have established your faithfulness in heaven itself.

February 2

A Wondrous Way

Dear Jesus,

You've taught me that the key to receiving is in giving and the way to success is servanthood. Having a humble attitude is superior to pride.

Your wisdom is available to every person. For me it started with knowing You as my Creator. Next I realized You make each individual for a definite purpose. I'm finding eternal happiness by following the path You've laid out for my life.

Jesus, You are Wondrous as is Your way. I celebrate You forever - my dwelling place, my truth and life!

Psalm 90:1-2
Lord, you have been our dwelling place throughout all generations. Before the mountains were born, or you brought forth the whole world, from everlasting to everlasting you are God.

February 3

Prophets

Dear Jesus,

Being a prophet is a peculiar occupation. What's required? Certainly the ability to survive the ups and downs of popularity. The pull of people pleasing needed to be renounced. You chose a few people as prophets who didn't want to accept Your call. Though reluctant, motivated by Your spirit, they finally conceded.

Often prophets endured horrendous rejection and hardships. No wonder they dreaded the responsibility of being Your spokesperson.

Some prophets had the task of instilling hope, but others proclaimed chastisement. I'm grateful to all who accepted Your call. Please protect every prophet in the world today who conveys Your truth. I'm mindful of those who speak among us now.

Jonah 2: 1-6
In my distress I [the prophet Jonah] called to the Lord, and He answered me. From deep in the realm of the dead I called for help, and You listened to my cry. You hurled me into the depths, into the very heart of the seas, and the currents swirled about me; all Your waves and breakers swept over me. I said, "I have been banished from your sight; yet I will look again toward Your holy temple." The engulfing waters threatened me, the deep surrounded me; but You, Lord my God, brought my life up from the pit.

February 4

Success and Failure

Dear Jesus,

I long to do Your will, but often I fail. I desire to trust You completely, but often doubt. Sometimes milliseconds separate the two. I love others, but rarely enough. I'm compassionate, but could be more so.

Jesus, I know You honor the humble and protect the honest. Infuse me with greater strength to be both. By Your Holy Spirit, guide me, Lord. Lead me to deeper goodness, to greater simplicity, to stronger integrity and to constant humility.

My life goes best when I recall this process of living is about honoring You. Jesus, may pleasing You be my highest motive and my primary goal every day. This is my heartfelt prayer.

Proverbs 11:2
When pride comes, then comes disgrace, but with humility comes wisdom.

February 5

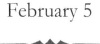

Fear

Dear Jesus,

An uncomfortable spirit of fear is disturbing me again wanting to suck away my peace, annoying me with its taunts, distressing me with what-ifs and threatening to trouble my sleep.

I know what to do. I am Your child. You want me free of all fear. I must shut my mind to anxiety and dread. Back to hell with these emotions!

Jesus, I will use the power and authority You've given me to banish every concern. Away with this crippling fear!

Psalm 22:19
But You, O Lord, do not be far from me: O My Strength, hasten to help me.

February 6

Darkness

Dear Jesus,

Sin is like choosing darkness while thinking I'm immersed in light. Sin is desiring what won't make me happy. It's like entering a dark doorway to loss, and walking a path to ultimate misery. I loathe sin. It's stupid to do what I know I shouldn't.

Yet, Jesus, how powerfully sin attracts! Satan tempts and distracts me well then sneers the second I succumb to his manipulations. He preys on my desire for accomplishment and lust for fine things. Activities riddled with pride may at first seem acceptable. Then they snatch away my peace and sear my soul. Jesus, You encourage me to repent. I know the desire to avoid sin must come first from me.

Please keep me alert to Satan's ploys. May my inner self always be turned toward Your will. Empower me to resist every urge to sin.

Matthew 7:13
Enter by the narrow gate, for wide is the gate and broad is the way that leads to destruction, and there are many who go in by it.

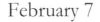

Fire or Smoke

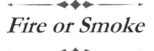

Dear Jesus,

I don't want to be a teeter-totter Christian. I've seen enough hypocrites in church, out of church. They're on holy fire or all smoke, turned on or turned off, on Your team, or standing on the sidelines.

To be honest Jesus, I've had moments of total trust in You and believing You are true and dependable. Other times I've questioned Your plans and wondered, where are You?

The choice is mine every day to either live confidently trusting You and being authentically me, or taking the teeter-totter ride. I can live in soul-searing connection with You or slide into doubt and fear. I need to stay fired up. It's awesome when my fire is divine, Holy Spirit ignited. I'm ready to burn. Let holy fire singe me. Jesus, help me burn strong always in You, for You, and through You.

Isaiah 12:2
Behold God is my salvation, I will trust and not be afraid; For the Lord is my strength and song; He also has become my salvation.

February 8

Responses

Dear Jesus,

I like to imagine the responses You stirred upon earth. What did the people You encountered think when You revealed Yourself as the glorious Restorer of Health, Source of Truth, and Maker of Men?

What did these people make of You -the leper who was embraced and healed, the boy who'd known death suddenly alive, and the Roman soldier trained to bow to Caesar overcome with allegiance to a new master? Jesus, You spoke of an old woman overjoyed in giving her all and a young woman freed from captivity no longer seeking phony love for coins.

Did praise simply burst from their mouths? Resplendent, magnificent, and full of delight. Did hearts thump, heads drop, and knees bend? Jesus, Restorer of Health and Source of Truth, the responses You stirred!

Matthew 11:4-6
Jesus replied, "Go back and report to John what you hear and see: The blind receive sight, the lame walk, those who have leprosy are cleansed, the deaf hear, the dead are raised and the good news is proclaimed to the poor."

February 9

Forever

Dear Jesus,

Forever is a word I can't fully comprehend. The idea is way too big for me.

How long is an eternal time period? This concept of unending time eludes me. All I know Lord is I've had glimpses of You in the present. You've probed my heart with Your tenderness, pierced my mind with Your holiness and flooded my soul completely with Your joy.

Experiencing You gives me the confidence to embrace the future with peace. It's enough for me to know that some day I'll be with You living in glory unending. Wherever with You is fine by me. I shall leave the details of forever to You. In the meantime please help me with every moment of now.

John 14:1-4
Jesus said, *"Do not let your hearts be troubled. You believe in God; believe also in Me. My Father's house has many rooms; if that were not so, would I have told you that I am going there to prepare a place for you? And if I go and prepare a place for you, I will come back and take you to be with Me that you also may be where I am. You know the way to the place where I am going."*

February 10

Stories

Dear Jesus,

The Bible tells fascinating stories about people. Some were kings who were sinners fathering sons who were saints. Stories tell of the rich and royal and the poor and unnamed. Weak, unwise youth and smart ones, too. The Bible contains drama to recall forever: Samson's hair, Gideon's torches of triumph, and Job's disasters. I also love the parables about pearls and yeast.

These stories make me think of a future story still unfolding. How will my life story read? I'd like a happy story Jesus, a love story and a success story. I know that's not always possible - I surrender the outcome to You.

What ending shall my story have? Whatever is okay as long as ultimately I'm embraced in Your arms. Until then, Jesus, keep me on track moment by moment, whatever my circumstances.

Hebrews 12:1-2
Therefore, since we are surrounded by such a great cloud of witnesses, let us throw off everything that hinders and the sin that so easily entangles. For the joy set before Him He endured the cross, scorning its shame, and sat down at the right hand of the throne of God.

February 11

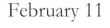

Control

Dear Jesus,

Controlling my thoughts and feelings can be hard. The truth is I wish You'd handle this completely Jesus instead of making me responsible for myself. But that's not realistic so I'll try my best.

Your Word says to cast every care upon You. I desire to respond with inner calm to every situation and not let myself become agitated. I need more self-discipline.

It's challenging to reject feelings of intimidation and fear and respond fearlessly to every challenge. I know You've given me this power. Now I must use it. At times mastering myself seems impossible, but Jesus, with Your grace I will.

Psalm 119:1-8
Blessed are those whose ways are blameless, who walk according to the law of the Lord. Blessed are those who keep His statutes and seek Him with all their heart—they do no wrong but follow His ways. You have laid down precepts that are to be fully obeyed.

February 12

Origin

Dear Jesus,

People wonder if humans were created by You supernaturally or if they evolved from nothing. I understand why this question of origin matters. Was every life planned or happenstance? I've studied the question extensively and have no doubt You're the Creator.

Evolutionists weave a web of words without scientific data using circular reasoning that misleads. Yet scientific facts are available and irrefutable. The unique, intricate DNA in every individual's complex cell structure can be viewed by electron microscopes. The complexity of every tiny cell is undeniable evidence that creation is impossible without design.

Jesus, how exciting to be created purposely with intention by You. Every person is a remarkable and amazing creation! I long for the day when all will know and worship You, awesome Creator.

Genesis 1:26
Then God said, "Let us make mankind in Our image, in Our likeness, so that they may rule over the fish in the sea and the birds in the sky, over the livestock and all the wild animals, and over all the creatures that move along the ground."

February 13

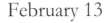

Folly

Dear Jesus,

The message of Your cross is considered sheer folly by many people. I understand why some say it's unreasonable for intelligent minds to think anyone would endure self-sacrifice to the point of death. Those heading toward perdition view the cross as absurd and don't feel a need of a Savior.

Your plan was for Your cross be a saving tool. Sadly Lord, Your cross has been denounced. The cross confounds the cleverness of the clever, the learning of the learned, and the philosophy of the philosophers. Folly lies with those who deny the message of Your cross. To be pitied are those who don't recognize its salvation power.

The cross appears foolishness to those who deny it, but Jesus, I believe with all my heart it is the exquisite wisdom of God.

Isaiah 29:14
Therefore once more I will astound these people with wonder upon wonder; the wisdom of the wise will perish, the intelligence of the intelligent will vanish.

February 14

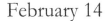

Heart Guard

Dear Jesus,

Gracious behavior is hard. When someone stabs me with unkindness, an ugly desire to strike back arises in me with fury. My heart attitude of peace easily shatters.

It's not an easy thing to control the heart. Within seconds my human emotions can switch. One minute I'm kind and thoughtful, the next I'm seeking personal attention and looking for what I can get, when I should be a fountain of giving.

Jesus, I know I'm loved by You with a mighty love and I desire to please You with a pure heart. Help me not take offense easily. Grace me with the power I need to display generosity and forgiveness in tough moments. May I have a heart like Yours.

Matthew 5:8
Blessed are the pure in heart, for they will see God.

February 15

Supernaturally

Dear Jesus,

Why settle for living naturally, when I can live supernaturally? Why live worldly with fretting and striving, when I can live otherworldly? Why live thoughtlessly, when I can live mindfully?

Why settle for less than what's great, when life holds so much more? Why limit myself to the ways of man, when I can experience the joys of God?

Why trouble myself with anxiety when I have You, the source of all peace? Why fear anything when I know You are merciful and trustworthy? Why indeed?

John 14:27
Lord You said, "Peace I leave with you; My peace I give you. I do not give to you as the world gives. Do not let your hearts be troubled and do not be afraid."

February 16

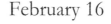

Covenants

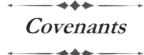

Dear Jesus,

The eternal covenants with You, old and new, are still valid today. Your Scripture says You'll do for me what You did for the Israelites in the days of Joshua. This amazes me!

You've given me a country to call home for which I did not labor. Cities and towns to enjoy that I did not build. I eat from fields I did not plant. Your covenant of love meets my every need.

All that's Yours is mine You tell me. My role is to avoid idols that seek to distract me and focus on serving You alone. Jesus, I'm honored to live out my covenant with You.

Joshua 24:14-18
Now fear the Lord and serve Him with all faithfulness. Throw away the gods your ancestors worshiped beyond the Euphrates River and in Egypt, and serve the Lord. But if serving the Lord seems undesirable to you, then choose for yourselves this day whom you will serve, whether the gods your ancestors served beyond the Euphrates, or the gods of the Amorites, in whose land you are living.

February 17

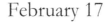

Reality

Dear Jesus,

Death comes to us all, but intellectually I can't completely comprehend that some day I'll walk the earth no more. May the reality of death pierce my mind. I want it to daily influence my thoughts and actions to help me live well. When the moment comes, may there be no past wrongs I neglected to right.

With the Psalmist David I want to say "I will bless You, Lord, while I live. For You're my ever-present help, my joy in life and hope in death." Jesus, prepare me for our eternal encounter.

I hope to go out strong, ever passionate with praise and aglow with Your brightness. I long to be faithful to my last breath, burning with Spirit-fire and lighting the paths of others toward You.

Psalm 63:4
I will praise You as long as I live, and in Your name I will lift up my hands.

February 18

One Alone

Dear Jesus,

My soul waits in silent prayer, in supreme submission to You alone. You're my high tower of protection. I have confidence in You every moment.

You're the Rock who keeps me immovable. I lift my hands in honor of Your name.

You're the One I adore. I refuse to waste time with second-best, pseudo gods. Nothing, no one but You Jesus, great source of all good for me. To You I cling. I yearn to see Your power and glory fully unleashed. With lips moving in praise I await the day.

1 John 4:16
And so we know and rely on the love God has for us. God is love. Whoever lives in love lives in God, and God in them.

February 19

Great Stone

Dear Jesus,

Scripture records the story of a great stone set in place by Joshua under an oak tree as a witness to people and a sign in Your Word for me today. This great stone was in the court of the Lord's sanctuary on the day Joshua made a covenant reminding people of Your love and power.

What a great idea to use this great stone as a symbol of covenant, lest the Israelites later deny they agreed to incline their hearts to You Lord: "The Lord our God we will serve; His voice we will obey."

In commemoration of the physical witness of the great stone I placed little stones in my garden plot. They remind me of my covenant promise to serve You with all my heart forever.

Joshua 24:27
"See!" he said to all the people. "This stone will be a witness against us. It has heard all the words the Lord has said to us. It will be a witness against you if you are untrue to your God."

February 20

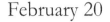

Rest

Dear Jesus,

People keep coming and going in my life, family and friends close to me and a few I scarcely know. Old friends, new friends. Each has a need for me to fill. Some also bring blessings to me.

At times the strain of people and hectic activity allows me little space for quiet and peace and I long for a deserted place and a slower pace. You often retreated to a quiet place for time with Your Father. Show me where I can find rest and peace.

Jesus, my Shepherd, create for me and within me a state of solitude. I need to be replenished by times of rest set apart with You.

Mark 6:30-32
The apostles gathered around Jesus and reported to Him all they had done and taught. Then, because so many people were coming and going that they did not even have a chance to eat, He said to them, "Come with Me by yourselves to a quiet place and get some rest." So they went away by themselves in a boat to a solitary place.

February 21

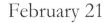

Shepherd

Dear Jesus,

How versatile You are in Your many amazing roles. You're a teacher of wondrous concepts, a multiplier of loaves and fishes, and a provider for our bodies and souls. You're the restorer of health, a great giver to all who approach You in need, and above all a shepherd who guides, when necessary going after anyone spiritually lost.

Jesus, You've given me roles I never expected. You've made me a vigilant shepherd of our family knowing when to prod and when to stand and watch. Help me lead our sheep to healthy grazing on truth and guard them courageously. Guiding involves sometimes admonishing and encouraging others for their good.

Teaching and shepherding my family requires frequent and extensive Sprit conversation. How grateful I am for Your help.

Isaiah 40:11
He tends His flock like a shepherd: He gathers the lambs in His arms and carries them close to His heart; He gently leads those that have young.

February 22

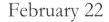

The Story

Dear Jesus,

Many hear the story of salvation, but are reluctant to believe it. Why? It seems strange and sad that the sacrificial death of one man can destroy the impact of sin.

To some it seems irrelevant, impossible even, that they should need a Savior in the first place. Do they recognize their jealousy, hatred or visible meanness? Surely they're not sinners, are they? Is sin even real? Overall their life's quite good, or is it?

May sinners hear again and finally believe the story of salvation from sin and entrance to heaven! May they recognize their sin and self-centeredness so the death-that-brings-life story becomes exciting and makes exquisite sense. Meaning, purpose, and salvation start with You, Lord. What an obvious difference You make in a life.

John 19:28-29
After this, Jesus, knowing that all things were now accomplished, that the Scripture might be fulfilled, said, "I thirst!" Now a vessel full of sour wine was sitting there; and they filled a sponge with sour wine, put it on hyssop, and put it to His mouth. So when Jesus had received the sour wine, He said, "It is finished!"

February 23

Passion

Dear Jesus,

My soul is thrilled as I gaze upon Your beautiful creation. Daily I give You praise. Your miracles never fail to amaze me. The words "I love You" sound far too ordinary for One so extraordinary!

The union of my soul with Your Spirit is a strong bond. The passion I feel for You is boundless. You are the great force that attracts and drives me. With You I feel as if I can ride upon clouds and wing among the stars.

My heart explodes with praise –this pure passion for You is the most beautiful kind. Jesus, I love You. May all I do honor You.

Psalm 89:14-18

Righteousness and justice are the foundation of Your throne; love and faithfulness go before You. Blessed are those who have learned to acclaim You, who walk in the light of Your presence, Lord. They rejoice in Your name all day long; they celebrate Your righteousness.

February 24

Man of Sorrows

Dear Jesus,

Man of Sorrows they called You, when they wounded You for my wrong deeds and chastised You without cause. You endured horrible pain to attain my good. Enemies whipped You with straps to appease my guilt. You remained silent before your tormentors so that I could live with joy forever.

Receptacle of all the world's guilt and carrier of my iniquities, You secured my healings and wholeness. You who had no sin assumed mine and all the world's - all the weight, pain and shame.

Jesus, how amazing that You would do this for me! I will spend all eternity immersed in gratitude.

Isaiah 53:3-6
He was despised and rejected by mankind, a man of suffering, and familiar with pain. Like One from whom people hide their faces He was despised, and we held Him in low esteem. Surely He took up our pain and bore our suffering, yet we considered Him punished by God, stricken by Him, and afflicted. But He was pierced for our transgressions, He was crushed for our iniquities; the punishment that brought us peace was on Him, and by His wounds we are healed.

February 25

Pretenders

Dear Jesus,

What were those men who played at being religious like? You knew them well – the Pharisees, pretenders, hypocrites. They put on a nice show, honoring You with their lips, but holding their hearts far off. Staying distant from You, outwardly they worshipped You showily, but their respect was without substance.

These pretenders clung to the tradition of men doing as they pleased, while telling others to observe Your Commandments. They murmured against Your truth, idolized human forefathers and savored their brief earthly power. Pharisees, pretenders, hypocrites! You told them, "Roast in Gehanna – hell."

Pretenders had no reason to blame You. The decision to believe was theirs. The decision to live Your way is individual to each of us. You know what I've chosen.

Matthew 23:13-15
Woe to you, teachers of the law and Pharisees, you hypocrites! You shut the door of the kingdom of heaven in people's faces. You yourselves do not enter, nor will you let those enter who are trying to. Woe to you, teachers of the law and Pharisees, you hypocrites!

February 26

Easy and Hard

Dear Jesus,

Being saved is simple. Living the saved life is a challenge. Declaring the truth of the Word of God is easy, applying it every day is hard. Experiencing Your love is simple. Living joyfully in the midst of difficult circumstances staying confident of Your love is challenging.

Interacting lovingly with unlovables isn't easy. Being in community with others is sometimes uncomfortable. Tending to the needs of others is often draining. The Christian life is joy and test. Easy and hard, hard and easy.

The challenge is great. The grace is greater. Thanks for making me aware and capable of the task, Lord.

James 2:14-17
What good is it, my brothers and sisters, if someone claims to have faith but has no deeds? Can such faith save them? Suppose a brother or a sister is without clothes and daily food. If one of you says to them, "Go in peace; keep warm and well fed," but does nothing about their physical needs, what good is it? In the same way, faith by itself, if it is not accompanied by action, is dead.

February 27

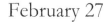

The Grip

Dear Jesus,

You gripped the twelve-year-old hand firmly of the young girl You'd snatched from death. Instantly the girl was up and walking about. The journey from death back to life leaves one hungry. You suggested she be given something to eat, lest her joy-filled parents forget her bodily needs.

You thought of everything and told her parents to tell no one about their daughter's return to life. You wanted the girl protected from people who might hound her with questions. After all what could she say except "I was lifeless, now I walk and breathe. I know not how, but I rejoice with all my heart."

Her father, the synagogue ruler, had been powerless to help his daughter. Frantic, desolate and desperate, he wisely sought out the miracle-working Son of God. The ruler didn't care who knew that he asked for Your help. Jesus, I too was dead, and touched by You. Now I live and move celebrating You, the Supreme Life-giver. I'm fine with all the world knowing.

Isaiah 41:13
For I am the Lord your God who takes hold of your right hand and says to you, Do not fear; I will help you.

February 28

Temples

Dear Jesus,

Does the business of religion sometimes make You weary? I admit it tires me. Building new churches, observing splitting churches, holding committee meetings and handling disagreements. I'm sure a certain amount of business must go on, but I fear it proceeds to excess at times and worship becomes less and less real.

Jesus, Your method seems ideal. You formed a training group of twelve and sent them out. You wanted Your message shared within small communities of believing hearts - families, households first.

Might there be too many physical temples called churches today and too few spiritual communities? I'm certainly not qualified to judge. I only know that I long to be a worthy spiritual temple as well as a holy servant within the physical church.

1 Corinthians 6:19
Do you not know that your bodies are temples of the Holy Spirit, who is in you, whom you have received from God? You are not your own.

February 29

Early Meeting

Dear Jesus,

You often awakened early and hurried off to the hills. The lure was exciting - being alone with the Father pulled You from sleep and drew You from the presence of Your beloved disciples. Jesus, You became energized for Your day in the renewing presence of the Father.

What might Your earthly life have been like had You neglected this morning meeting?

I too feel the Father's pull as my eyes greet morning and I rush to our meeting. May I remember when my bed seems sweet that the benefits of being alone with the Father far outweigh the brief pleasure of sleep. Days when I fail to be alone in Your presence are powerless and disjointed. I treasure our early morning meeting.

Mark 1:35
Very early in the morning, while it was still dark, Jesus got up, left the house and went off to a solitary place, where He prayed.

March 1

Spirit

Dear Jesus,

I'd like to have been there when Your Holy Spirit appeared to the terrified group assembled in the Upper Room. How incredible to hear mighty sounds from heaven and see tongues resembling flames of fires separate and settle on each person present.

Oh how I'd love to hear the music of many languages pouring from tongues and telling everyone about the greatness of God!

Holy Spirit, fully present in this moment, re-create Your fire and music in me now. Diffuse it throughout my soul. May I be as determined as the disciples present at the first Pentecost to speak boldly so that all may know and exalt You and Your mighty works.

Acts 2:1-4
When the day of Pentecost came, they were all together in one place. Suddenly a sound like the blowing of a violent wind came from heaven and filled the whole house where they were sitting. They saw what seemed to be tongues of fire that separated and came to rest on each of them. All of them were filled with the Holy Spirit and began to speak in other tongues as the Spirit enabled them.

March 2

Needing People

Dear Jesus,

The Gospels record a time when You ordered the hungry people following You to sit in groups of fifty before you multiplied the loaves and fishes. Then Your disciples moved among them to distribute their meal. Why this division of Your followers? Was it to teach me that being in small groups is a good thing?

I search for genuine Christian community. I want to be with people who are truly Yours, not just in name but lifestyle. What shall I look for?

You say, seek individuals who live with gladness and simplicity, generosity and steadfastness. Find people given to heartfelt praise, who exhibit singleness of spiritual devotion to You. Avoid indifferent and frivolous people. Seek out those with unfailing integrity who are eager to conform to Your Father's will. These are signs of those who are Yours, who truly live the Christian journey and speak Your truth.

Hebrews 10:24-25
And let us consider how we may spur one another on toward love and good deeds, not giving up meeting together, as some are in the habit of doing, but encouraging one another—and all the more as you see the Day approaching.

March 3

In Control

Dear Jesus,

You know me perfectly. You know I enjoy being in control. I like to keep the structure of my days a certain way. I desire Your will of course, but frankly I prefer the parts that fit nicely with my plans. I enjoy picking and choosing and could I skip the faith tests please?

Jesus, I can imagine You laughing. Certainly I'm not being realistic so go ahead and have Your way. I'll try not to grumble. You know that sometimes I fail to see and savor good in all the circumstances You allow for me.

I need Your help. Please don't let me mess up. Acceptance of Your will, Your plan and Your law minus my selfish desires is non-negotiable. This truly is my deepest desire.

Psalm 119:165
Great peace have those who love Your law, and nothing can make them stumble.

March 4

Paul

Dear Jesus,

Paul was blinded in an instant and frightened beyond belief when You appeared to Him. I'd like to have seen his expression when You asked, "Why do you persecute Me?"

In an instant his allegiance changed forever. Never again would Christianity seem false to him. Then troubles came fast and furious. Physical danger became commonplace. Still he lived each moment joyfully, plunged through pain and persisted. He was a non-complainer to the nth degree and His confidence in You never wavered. He knew You set him free to be a good news carrier to others. He said, "For me to live is Christ."

Jesus, I share Paul's conviction. I know You are the Son of God and I want all the world to know. I long to display Paul's courage in boldly proclaiming who You are.

Acts 22:6-10a
About noon as I [Paul]came near Damascus, suddenly a bright light from heaven flashed around me. I fell to the ground and heard a voice say to me, "Saul! Saul! Why do you persecute me?" "Who are you, Lord?" I asked. "I am Jesus of Nazareth, whom you are persecuting," He replied. "What shall I do, Lord?" I asked. "Get up," the Lord said, "and go into Damascus."

March 5

Holy Fire

Dear Jesus,

Persistent faith is like a fire spreading everywhere. Good fire, warming fire, healing fire. That's what Holy Spirit fire is. Holy fire can be walked through without getting burned. It's like the fire that burned spontaneously for Elijah when he demonstrated God's power for the people.

Bad fire is doubt, rebellion and lack of faith. It's killing fire, destroying fire, like the fire of hell that can't be quenched.

Jesus, may Your Spirit fire burn bright in me forever. Keep me blazing with faith. May my glowing embers illuminate You to others. Holy fire is my desire.

Psalm 66:12
You [Lord] let people ride over our heads; we went through fire and water, but You brought us to a place of abundance.

March 6

Hupomone and Makrophumia

Dear Jesus,

I know You're a word lover. You used words with such precision. After all, You are the Word of God. I found Hupomone and makrophumia - two big Greek words in the Bible. "Hupomone" is defined as cheerful endurance, patience, and an inner ability to keep going. The Greek word "makrophumia" means calmness in the face of suffering and adversity, forbearance or fortitude, longsuffering, patience and good-natured tolerance of delay. All good qualities!

These Greek words inspire me. I like easy, orderly direction for life's problems and quick answers to annoying questions. That's not always possible. Hupomone and makrophumia help me when I must go beyond my usual endurance.

Jesus, it's Your grace that helps me bear up under hardship and put up with difficult people. Give me lots of hupomone and makrophumia please.

Hebrews 12:1
Therefore, since we are surrounded by so great a cloud of witnesses, let us also lay aside every weight, and sin which clings so closely, and let us run with hupomone (cheerful endurance) the race that is set before us.

March 7

Four Evangelists

Dear Jesus,

I wonder if the authors of the Gospels, Matthew, Mark, Luke and John, ever thought they'd be read by millions of people and become famous forever. Copies of their Gospels are found all around the world. How delightful to think they never knew or even considered the longevity of their fame. Assuredly, they never even cared.

Because it wasn't about fame, was it? Nor numbers who heard or read, but only following Your will Jesus. They were spurred by compulsion born of love. They lived with the burning desire to record Your life and work because You're the One who led them to the Father.

May I be single-minded also Jesus alongside all those privileged to handle the truth about You.

The Gospels of *Matthew, Mark, Luke and John*

March 8

The Children

Dear Jesus,

When You walked the earth You often placed Your holy hands upon children in blessing. You scolded the disciples when they complained about You giving Your time to attending to these little ones. They wanted the children kept away from You.

You admired aloud their simple faith. The children sensed Your authenticity and eagerly flocked to You with total trust. Your disciples learned that You valued every individual at any age.

Jesus, may I be like these little children, eager for every encounter with You. May I accept all Your plans for me with child-like joy and trust.

Matthew 19:12-14
Then people brought little children to Jesus for Him to place His hands on them and pray for them. But the disciples rebuked them. Jesus said, "Let the little children come to Me, and do not hinder them, for the kingdom of heaven belongs to such as these."

March 9

Down

Dear Jesus,

The truth is I'm down at this moment. I dislike admitting it, but life is harder than I'd like. My relationships aren't going well. I'm feeling bruised by the world's pressures and weary of what appears to be the devil's thrusts. I can't deny these emotions by saying everything's fine. Not when my flesh wants to quit.

Jesus, I'm praying You'll renew my energy and soothe my heart. Out of my desperation, I call to You. My mind's in a swirl, yet my faith is strong as can be. I know You'll help me persevere. Please be quick, I pray.

I'm confident a joy-filled Kingdom lifestyle will be mine again. May I bring You glory even during this difficult time. Help me remember that even this sadness shall soon pass.

Ephesians 1:3 & 4
Blessed be the God and Father of our Lord Jesus Christ, who has blessed us in Christ with every spiritual blessing in the heavenly places, just as He chose us in Christ before the foundation of the world to be holy and blameless before Him in love.

March 10

Gloom and Grief

Dear Jesus,

In Scripture I read about the gloom and grief of the rich young man who walked away clutching his great possessions and abandoning heaven's treasures. Gloom and grief became his companions, rather than the joy and delight You desired to lavish upon him.

His decision seems foolish to me. Yet how often do I covet material things and fall for Satan's lies by holding too tightly to my stuff? Plus I often cling to mental obsessions like guilt, bitterness, and revenge. How quickly I can abandon my true delight, disrupt my peace and lose the treasure of a holy, clear mind.

Jesus, I will refuse to allow gloom and grief to pervade my spirit. The choice of priorities for how I live is mine. I choose Your way and joy. Gloom and grief be gone.

2 Corinthians 5:1
For we know that if the earthly tent we live in is destroyed, we have a building from God, a house not made with hands, eternal in the heavens.

March 11

Whole Heart

Dear Jesus,

With all my heart, all my soul, all my life force, all my mind, and all my strength - physical, emotional, spiritual - with all I am - I will love You always, oh Jesus, my Lord, my God.

Wholeheartedly will I serve You. Forever will I glorify You, Jesus, my Lord. Because of You I bravely enter new situations knowing I'm never alone, unloved, or unprotected. I'm blessed at every age with Your beauty of holiness.

You'll have nothing less than my whole heart always.

Psalm 116:12-14
What shall I return to the Lord for all His goodness to me? I will lift up the cup of salvation and call on the name of the Lord. I will fulfill my vows to the Lord in the presence of all His people.

March 12

Trinity

Dear Jesus,

How awesome that as Father, Son, Spirit, You are love, love, love. Three names, three persons in one Triune God. What a mystery to contemplate Your existence. Triune God, trice sovereign, triple glorious.

All three Persons, unique and complete, in a love relationship with one another and with me! Theologians have tried for years to explain how this can be.

My mind can't comprehend the mystery either but my heart acknowledges its reality. My belief is based on my amazing experience of You. Sharpen my senses and enhance my awareness continually that I may properly honor the treasure of You, my beloved Triune God.

Luke 24:49
[Jesus said] "I am going to send you what My Father has promised; but stay in the city until you have been clothed with power from on high."

March 13

Master Physician

Dear Jesus,

My physical health is occasionally poor and at times fails me completely. During these times hope eludes me. Then I beseech You, my Master Physician. Although it sometimes seems a long wait to my impatient body, in the rightness of time, You answer.

You bandage my hurts with spiritual silk. You banish my terror with touches of Your invisible hand and make me strong and healthy again. Other times You use the expertise of the wise doctors You've gifted with healing heads and hands.

Jesus, how I praise You for ministering to me physically as well as spiritually!

Malachi 4:2
But for you who revere My name, the sun of righteousness will rise with healing in its rays. And you will go out and frolic like well-fed calves.

March 14

Accounts

Dear Jesus,

In Scripture, You tell about a master who asks his servants how much they made buying and selling using what You entrusted to them. The man with ten mina made ten. His reward was authority over ten cities. Another man with ten mina made five and his reward was authority over five cites. Another man with ten mina made nothing because he feared the harshness of the master if he lost it.

To his shock, the man who did nothing with his investment had what he held taken from him and given to the man with the most profit from his efforts. Each man was judged by his actions. So shall I be.

Jesus, I promise not to hoard your gifts. On the day when You ask for an accounting from me I pray You'll find immense value in my account.

Matthew 25:14-19
For the kingdom of heaven is like a man traveling to a far country, who called his own servants and delivered his goods to them. And to one he gave five talents, to another two, and to another one, to each according to his own ability; and immediately he went on a journey.

March 15

Witnesses

Dear Jesus,

I consider it a privilege to speak about You. My lips delight in telling Your deeds. My feet are ready to walk wherever You send me to tell about Your wondrous ways. My knees were created for worship of You. On earth below and heaven above, I long for everyone to know You're the son of Man, and the God of everything, now and forever.

Jesus, I'll speak Your Name boldly and tell of Your deeds until the day I see Your face. I add my voice to the many souls in Scripture lifted in witness of You because You are worthy.

I'm thrilled to join with Your holy angels in praising you while yet on earth.

Psalm 25:3-5
No one who hopes in You will ever be put to shame, but shame will come on those who are treacherous without cause. Show me Your ways, Lord, teach me Your paths. Guide me in Your Truth and teach me, for You are God my Savior, and my hope is in You all day long.

March 16

Oops

Dear Jesus,

My mind is stuck in oops and oh-no's. The things I've done and shouldn't have done and the things I didn't do and should have. You know the hurts I've given to others and the hurts I've felt. Jesus, I need to get unstuck. Help me please!

In Scripture, I read about King David's oops and they comfort me. The story of Paul's travail of ouches strengthens me. David's repentance and renewed sanctity reassures me. Jonah's movement forward after his foolish sin charges me up. Peter's changed heart inspires me afresh.

The Biblical heroes didn't get stuck in their past oops but became victors. And so will I! I appreciate these human examples in Your Word! Hope surges through me when I read about others overcoming failures and obstacles. Through Your holy stories in Scripture my mind gets renewed and I come unstuck. Praise You!

Romans 6:11-12
Likewise you also reckon yourselves to be dead to sin, but alive to God in Christ Jesus Our Lord. Therefore do not let sin reign in your mortal body, that you should obey its lusts.

March 17

Morning Moments

Dear Jesus,

I love our early morning moments together before the commitments of the day call me forth. My prayer is purposeful, soothing and exciting. I begin with gratitude, the best gift I can give. I recall Holy Spirit urges that have given my life direction. I remember accidents and illnesses survived, and miraculous healings. Praise bubbles up and bursts through me.

These morning moments are my daily tool, keeping me sharp and effective. They take less than an hour, not much time, but enrich all the rest of my day. Time with You doesn't consume my energy, it expands it.

The words of my morning prayer are: "Jesus, I know You're with me in every situation. Give me Divine Wisdom word-by-word and act-by-act. I await expectantly what You'll do. I'm humbled and thankful to start every day with You as we journey through life together."

Psalm 139:9-10
If I take the wings of the morning, and dwell in the uttermost parts of the sea, even there Your hand shall lead me, and Your right hand shall hold me.

March 18

Carefree

Dear Jesus,

I become stressed easily by ordinary happenings of life. When I'm over-anxious, impatient and troubled with care, help me remember You make me strong and capable. Every need is supplied by You, my Lord.

Often I lack patience during trials, but there are times when I must be patient. Please help me wait with expectation and trust. That nasty Satan entices me to a sense of futility, despair and frustration.

Jesus, give me power to respond to any situation with faith and confidence. Your love never fails. In every act requiring trust and patience I want to be like the lily, totally confident and carefree because of You. With Your help I can be.

Luke 12:27
Consider the lilies, how they grow: they neither toil nor spin; and yet I say to you, even Solomon in all his glory was not arrayed like one of these.

March 19

True Treasure

Dear Jesus,

Thank you Jesus for teaching me how to rightly order my wants and desires. Possessions rust and rot before human eyes while greed screams for more.

Jesus, I prefer the inexhaustible kind of treasure, free from decay, safe from thieves. I believe it pleases You to give me the joy of anticipating the Kingdom of heaven while I still walk the soil of earth.

My heart is content with You, my true treasure throughout my life journey. On the day my soul is called to heaven, I know the things I once held dear will mean nothing.

Ezra 7:10
For Ezra had prepared his heart to seek the Law of the Lord, and to do it, and to teach statutes and ordinances in Israel.

March 20

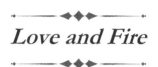

Love and Fire

Dear Jesus,

When I think of You, earth around me dims, awe descends, and my human pride disappears. I become breathless at the thought of Your sacrifice of love for me. I'm inspired to carry Your love forth.

You loved by giving Yourself as God's only Son, greatly beloved. Because I love You I give my words, my time, and my all to You and for You.

Is this what it means to be on fire for You, Jesus? Simple words, love and fire, involving passion. They require a willingness to go beyond love layer one, ever deeper, always finding newness and joy in You. And I do.

Psalm 62:5-8
Yes, my soul, find rest in God; my hope comes from Him. Truly He is my rock and my salvation; He is my fortress, I will not be shaken. My salvation and my honor depend on God; He is my mighty rock, my refuge. Trust in Him at all times, you people; pour out your hearts to Him, for God is our refuge.

March 21

Gratitude

Dear Jesus,

What better way to spend time than by telling You continually how grateful I am for my life and for all the plans You've ordained. I'm mindful of my many healings and also Your many rescues for me and those I love.

Most of all, I'm grateful that You've given me a mind that comprehends who You are and understands who I am in relationship to You.

You've given me a strong body with a healthy mind and above all, a soul infused with love. I'm fire-born for Spirit work, designed by You for this time in history. Thank You, my awesome Lord for the privilege of knowing and loving You.

John 21:25
And there are also many other things that Jesus did, which, if they were written one by one, I suppose not even the world itself could contain the books that would be written.

March 22

Holy and Brave

Dear Jesus,

There is no one like You. You're Divine goodness and holiness. Courage dwells within You and flows from You. You ignite me with sparks of love. My holiness comes from being in Your presence. I'm humbled that You occasionally allow me the awesome privilege of glimpsing Your activity among men.

I'm privileged to be one of Your present-day followers who are able to serve You like Your faithful servants of old. I praise You for their examples.

I accept all the circumstances You allow for me, even the painful ones. When I experience suffering, You give me courage and assurance that all pain will end some day, although perhaps not on earth. You grace me Jesus to remain holy and brave in the here and now.

Leviticus 21: 8
Regard them as holy, because they offer up the food of your God. Consider them holy, because I the Lord am holy—I who make you holy.

March 23

Shield and Sword

Dear Jesus,

Where are my shield and sword? My shield of faith is necessary to defend others from spiritual marauders prowling about. Knowledge of the Word is my holy sword. Study of Scripture prepares my soul for the onslaught, which surely comes. Holy Spirit equip me for this battle.

Satan and his minions are relentless. Jesus, strengthen my spiritual bones and muscles. Unaided I tend to be weak, wavering and bend too easily. Jesus with You I'm assured of ultimate victory every time.

Together with You I can quench all the darts of the evil one.

Ephesians 6:16
Above all, taking the shield of faith with which you will be able to quench all the fiery darts of the wicked one.

March 24

The Parables

Dear Jesus,

The parables in Scripture are short, pithy gems that pierce my mind with Your truth. Applying their principles to my life is essential.

Jesus, probe my heart for holy motives. I want to sweep away any internal mental debris so that only Your pearls may be found. I long to plant the mustard seed with expectation, be the virgin with endless oil and wake the judge with my persistent pounding.

Divine Parable-Speaker and Ultimate Truth-Teacher may my diligent commitment to Your principles endure. I long for the day when all the world knows and worships You.

Matthew 13:35
That it might be fulfilled which was spoken by the prophet, saying: "I will open My mouth in parables; I will utter things kept secret from the foundation of the world."

March 25

Correction

Dear Jesus,

I understand that correcting me is a sign of Your concern for me. I don't enjoy it, but I need it. Tough thought, but true. Correction draws me closer and conforms me to You Jesus. Correction helps me avoid sins that quench Your Spirit.

Correction happens in several ways: through admonishments of Scripture and from suggestions made by Christian friends. I also receive correction directly from Your Holy Spirit.

Correction often hurts, but I know it helps me. Jesus, I welcome correction, even embrace it because it's for my good. Prune and correct me with Your love.

Hebrews 12: 5-6
My son, do not take the Lord's discipline lightly, or faint when you are reproved by Him, for the Lord disciplines the one He loves, and punishes every son whom He receives.

March 26

One Voice

Dear Jesus,

My voice speaks prayers aloud and sings praises. My voice of confession purges my failings and pettiness. My spoken words offer forgiveness to others when I'm offended.

Negatively, my voice can often spring too quickly to my self-defense. It can be too eager to speak complaints and selfishly insist on my plan. My voice can either encourage others or singe others.

One voice, one choice I have to use for You, Jesus or to submerge in the depths of myself. Jesus, may the gift of my voice be used as intended - to glorify You.

Song of Songs 2:14
...show me your face, let me hear your voice; for your voice is sweet, and your face is lovely.

March 27

Faith Crisis

Dear Jesus,

Are You saddened by people who verbally attack You? I observe a typical pattern - when something bad happens like sickness, financial loss or death people complain, "Where were You? Why didn't You stop this?"

These people think life shouldn't have problems. Why do they have to deal with difficulties? The fact is earth isn't heaven and terrible things often do happen to people. Earth is the domain of hellish power. And why should anyone be immune? Is expecting a smooth, easy life perhaps evidence of human pride?

Whatever life brings, there's always a refuge, a place of trust and security. Whatever happens Jesus, You offer comfort, strength and support. I've experienced this repeatedly – it's true.

Hebrews 12: 14
Pursue peace with everyone, and holiness – without it no one will see the Lord.

Your Child

Dear Jesus,

You call me Yours. You delight me with joy. I love being Your child and receiving Your awesome favor as we journey through life together. Praise You! Whatever the future holds I need...
Only to pause,
Only to listen,
Only to think,
Only to heart-speak,
Because You'll be present, armed with the arsenal of heaven to work on my behalf.
And You tell me I can expect to experience amazing things...
Strength with joy,
Peace not chaos,
Wisdom through simplicity,
Love instead of hate,
Because You will be present to empower me.

Luke 1:19
The angel answered, "I am Gabriel, who stands in the presence of God, and I was sent to speak to you and tell you this good news."

March 29

Providing

Dear Jesus,

You told Your disciples to give the hungry people who had followed You something to eat. The disciples were astounded that starving people could possibly be fed when they lacked financial resources! Jesus, Your order was clear. Your expectation that they could provide sustenance shocked these men even before Your amazing multiplication of food.

Your disciples recognized the human need for food, but were ready to send people away to get it elsewhere. Elsewhere is here, You said, for those who follow You. The miraculous power needed for provision was available then and still is now.

So, too, empowered by You, I can give others what they need and meet physical and spiritual needs. What a precious responsibility and privilege to be a provider!

Mark 6:37
"You give them something to eat," He [Jesus] responded.

March 30

Divine Connection

Dear Jesus,

Connection with You has splendid benefits available to anyone who follows You. I treasure the privilege of hearing Your tender love messages spoken straight into my heart. Because of our relationship I live with abundant joy. I'm grateful for Your direction in my life through Your Word and prompts of the Holy Spirit. Your guidance spares me disgrace and protects me from foolish behaviors.

Long ago I acknowledged You as only a distant force. Now I've come to know You personally. Who knew true ecstasy exists and could only be found in You!

I can best describe our friendship as mercy-washed and grace-tinged. I treasure our divinely energized connection.

Romans 8:31
What then are we to say about these things? If God is for us, who is against us?

March 31

Never Before

Dear Jesus,

I've never known a love like Yours before. There never-will-be another like You in my life, You're my never-disappointing God.

Your concern is always tender. Your correction always constructive and Your intervention always timely. You bathe me in security and enable me to walk with passionate purpose. You set me upon a stable foundation. You surround me with unseen spiritual guards.

You have perfect wisdom, power and love. You're my always-perfect God. I gulp with awe and honor you every day with fervent prayer.

Psalm 41:13
May the Lord, the God of Israel be praised from everlasting to everlasting. Amen and amen.

April 1

Transformed

Dear Jesus,

My world seems gray today. I look into Scripture for a glimpse of brightness. I need to sense a word, a hint of Your presence Lord.

I absorb the words of truth in the Bible and experience Your heart revealed in these Biblical principles. Soon Your Word transforms me. I finish reading and look up. The sun is visible again in my world You are truly the living Word. Not a man speaking only words of love, but fully God with divine messages of real love.

It means so much to know that You're a real and personal God, not a specter in the sky, impossible of being pleased. I don't place my hope in a haughty, distant ruler or expect power from a pretense. You're the one and only, real and personal God.

John 1:1
In the beginning was the Word and the Word was with God and the Word was God.

April 2

Roman Truth

Dear Jesus,

The book of Romans in the Bible contains exciting facts about Your Holy Spirit. Romans 8:9 says the Spirit of God dwells in me! Romans 5:5 states that the Holy Spirit pours out the love of God in my heart. Romans 5:26 assures me the Holy Spirit helps me in my weaknesses and intercedes for me with sounds that can't be uttered.

Because of Your Holy Spirit I don't walk totally in the flesh - Romans 8:1. I live and move according to Your Holy Spirit. Romans 8:2 says the law of the Spirit has set me free from sin and death. Romans 8:5 reminds me to keep my mind focused on Your Spirit.

In Romans 8:23 I read that the Holy Spirit has sealed me as Your own and gifts me with multiple fruits and gifts. By the power of Your Holy Spirit I'm able to live in victory. Romans 8:16 reminds me that Your Holy Spirit bears witness that I am God's child!

Romans 8:28
And we know that in all things God works for the good of those who love Him, who have been called according to His purpose.

April 3

One Time

Dear Jesus,

I have only this time, one lifetime to fulfill my purpose and one opportunity to impact current culture. May I be like a Gideon against the Midianites, a Moses to the masses, an Esther who rescues my people and like a Paul revealing Your truth to the Gentiles.

Jesus, You've instilled divine confidence in me. I know Your Holy Spirit supernaturalizes my efforts. Boldly I go forward. You created me for this time in history. I'm humbled and excited.

I know these goals sounds lofty. Use me as You will. I'm content to be simply, authentically your ambassador to my circle of acquaintances. So may we all.

Matthew 24:19
Go therefore, and make disciples of all nations, baptizing them in the name of the Father and of the Son and of the Holy Spirit, teaching them to observe everything I have commanded you.

April 4

Attacks

Dear Jesus,

What You endured at the hands of attackers! Your once-holy temple of worship was desecrated before Your eyes. What anger this must have stirred within You. Your physical body of human flesh was tortured and ravished. No one has ever been attacked like You. Yet You endured it all.

You, the supreme hater of sin, who will ultimately destroy every evil controlled Your fury through all these attacks. I too am angered at the evil around me. May I show pity and demonstrate patience even as I long for evil-doing to cease.

How I await the day when harmony, love and peace fill every heart and the world is transformed.

Romans 1:18
The wrath of God is being revealed from heaven against all the godlessness and wickedness of people, who suppress the truth by their wickedness.

April 5

Everything

Dear Jesus,

Everything good comes from You. Whatever delight my eyes see, whatever goodness my hand touches and whatever wonders my mind perceives come to me as Your gift.

You empower all human accomplishments. Because of You I'm able to bless others through my gifts as they bless me with theirs. Directly and indirectly You bless us with all that is good.

All through You, my Lord and God. You are the Great Gift-Giver and Amazing Good-Giver. I can never stop exalting You!

Psalm 34:3
Proclaim with me the Lord's greatness; let us exalt His name together.

April 6

Vital Messages

Dear Jesus,

It's intriguing to consider the amazing messages delivered by angels and their helpful works among humans.

Angel to Joseph: Protect Mary and my Spirit-conceived child.

Angel to wise men: King Herod mustn't find the Christ-child born to be king.

Angel to Joseph: Danger developing, take your family and flee.

Angel to Joseph: Move again for safety.

I'm comforted Jesus to know that You send angels to aid us. How awesome!

Exodus 23:20
See, I am sending an angel ahead of you to guard you along the way and to bring you to the place I have prepared.

April 7

Women of Sin

Dear Jesus,

How amazing that women of sin can live holy, useful lives once they repent and are transformed by Your grace.

Rahab, a harlot, became a rescuer of God's people. Bathsheba, with whom King David sinned, mothered Solomon, who later became King. All were in Your lineage Jesus. Mary Magdalene, woman of ill repute, was the first person spoken to by You after Your Resurrection.

Jesus, You're the Amazing Life-Changer. How encouraging to know sin-filled women can become free and become a blessing to others. I wish I were perfect, but I know I'm not. Yet even sin-filled me can be used by You.

Joshua 6:25
And Joshua spared Rahab the harlot, her father's household, and all that she had. So she dwells in Israel to this day, because she hid the messengers whom Joshua sent to spy out Jericho.

April 8

Joseph

Dear Jesus,

You selected Joseph to be the earthly father of Jesus. Certainly, it was a wise choice, but how did you pick this man privileged to protect Mary as she carried Your human and divine life? What made Joseph worthy to help raise You as a baby, then train You as a youth, You the Son of God?

Of course, You kept close watch over Joseph and his family. Twice angels appeared to guide him. You provided all the help Joseph needed as You do for me.

Whatever made Joseph capable as a parent, may it be in me as I nurture the children You've given to my husband and me. We long to be a godly family honoring You.

Matthew 1:19-20

Then Joseph her husband, being a just man, and not wanting to make her a public example, was minded to put her away secretly. But while he thought about these things, behold, an angel of the Lord appeared to him in a dream, saying, Joseph, son of David, do not be afraid to take to you Mary your wife, for that which is conceived in her is of the Holy Spirit.

April 9

Crosses

Dear Jesus,

The cross isn't a popular idea. Many abhor the thought that You were crucified. Why should such sacrifice be necessary? Wasn't it premature to end Your presence on earth at age thirty-three? You were clearly needed here, then and now.

Some say Godhood shouldn't have had to submit to man's abuse. Since Your supernatural power is real, Jesus, You could have used it at any moment to abolish this evil. Why did it have to be the agonizing cross that brought eternal life? I understand this was part of the Divine plan, so who am I to question. No cheap salvation had power to loose the chains of death upon man.

I accept this mystery and embrace the cross even though it's unfathomable. I'm resolved to struggle with my own crosses although I'd prefer to set them aside. Saints struggled to find strength to endure and so will I!

Hebrews 12:2
Looking unto Jesus, the author and finisher of our faith, who for the joy that was set before Him endured the cross, despising the shame, and has sat down at the right hand of the throne of God.

April 10

Eternal Life

Dear Jesus,

Some scientists believe death is the end of human life and hope in eternity is false. Faith asserts when our earthly life ceases our eternal existence begins. Science has some facts, but not all truth. Reason and faith can work together. Natural and supernatural truth do not contradict one another when filtered through wisdom.

Many scientific authorities say it's foolish not to believe in You and in eternal life! They don't accept blind opinions and recognize that even science points to You.

Jesus, I totally agree because I've personally experienced Your reality.

John 8:32
You shall know the Truth and the Truth will set you free.

April 11

Interactions

Dear Jesus,

The ideal ways for human interactions are clearly set forth in Your Word. We have a choice. Human focus or Yours? A selfish life or an other-centered life? What shall it be?

I can easily lapse into self-centeredness, valuing myself too highly and reeking of personal pride. This alienates others and blocks my compassion and mercy.

Help me remember haughtiness and judging are never right. Forgiveness is always called for. Humble godly behavior is best. Praying for others is the most powerful way to bless.

Luke 6: 37
Do not judge, and you will not be judged. Do not condemn, and you will not be condemned. Forgive, and you will be forgiven.

April 12

Mystery

Dear Jesus,

It's a great mystery how You can dwell at the right Hand of the Father in heavenly realms and dwell in me at this moment. You dwell in my moments of darkness as well as times of joy. How wonderful that You live out Your divine life within me.

Truly I don't understand, but I believe it's true. I've experienced our intimate closeness. Me in You and You in me. It's a connection like none other.

Jesus, all creation is sustained through You by Your Holy Spirit. You initiate and maintain all truth and beauty. Do I really understand what this means? Probably not, but with all my mind and heart I believe.

2 Peter 1:3
As His divine power has given to us all things that pertain to life and godliness, through the knowledge of Him who called us by glory and virtue…

April 13

Titles

Dear Jesus,

What I love, Jesus, is thinking about Who You are. I delight in finding titles to describe Your majesty. You're my Triune God of Creation, Exalted God of Revelation. You're My Living Temple, Awesome Covenant-Maker and Faithful Covenant-Keeper.

Jesus, You're My Fierce Defender, Demon-Destroying Savior. Most importantly of all You're the Fullness of God and Righteousness-restoring Son of God.

All these things and more You are to me and everyone who seeks You. You've made Yourself available to every generation.

Colossians 1:19
For God was pleased to have all His fullness dwell in Him.

April 14

Safe & Free

Dear Jesus,

In my mind, I often dance with moonbeams and observe Your world with wonder. I'm delighted with Your laws of nature and the personal freedom You give me. I live confidently in Your truth. I flit fearlessly through my life with You my Jesus, my Love, and my All.

Jesus, when I walk through danger I see smoke. Some blazes I spark accidentally, others ignite from uncontrollable circumstances. The flames are often fierce. Yet I walk bravely through.

I can endure anything with You Jesus, my protector, my love and my all.

Isaiah 43: 1-3
When you pass through the waters, I will be with you; and when you pass through the rivers, they will not sweep over you. When you walk through the fire, you will not be burned; the flames will not set you ablaze.

April 15

Real Love

Dear Jesus,

How awesome that Your eyes are upon my ways and Your face shines upon me. Your heart is filled with love for me. Your feet go before me figuratively smoothing my way. Your lips speak my instructions and the light of Your grace rests upon my life.

Because of Your loving ways toward me, I honor You alone. I think of you as the architect of my life on earth and in heaven, the destroyer of my daily demons, and gracious giver of every good thing I have. You're the One-Alone-Man-and-God. You're above, around, and all about - always near. What joy!

Jesus, when I want to visualize real love, I think of You. When I want to internalize peace, I think of You. When I long to contemplate truth, I think of You. When I want to personalize goodness, I think of You. When I want to meditate on perfection, my mind focuses on You, my precious Lord.

Job 22:28
What you decide on will be done; and light will shine on your ways.

April 16

Your Name

Dear Jesus,

In the Old Testament people didn't even dare to speak Your name. Now You've given me the privilege of speaking it constantly. I call upon Your Name in times of difficulty or danger. I fall asleep saying Jesus over and over.

At the sound of Your Name, my fingers fly across this keyboard with phrases of praises. My mind spins with holy thoughts. The thought of Your Name makes my soul sing.

I'm saddened that Your Name is often spoken carelessly by others in moments of anger, exasperation or desperation. How grievous it must be to You to hear Yourself disrespected. I long for that day when all people will say the name Jesus, the Holiest of words, with reverence and awe.

Exodus 20: 6-8
You shall not misuse the name of the Lord your God, for the Lord will not hold anyone guiltless who misuses His Name.

April 17

Perception

Dear Jesus,

You tell me to be perceptive as I view the details in my world. Otherwise it's easy to miss much of what You intend for me to see.

You open my heart wide so that I won't miss the hurting waiter in need of an extra tip given with caring words, "I don't know why but God has told me to double your tip today as a gift from Him because He loves You." The older woman pushing her grocery cart, lingering at the deli aisle who's in need of conversation. The maintenance worker in the restroom who's never been thanked for her work before.

You show me three white butterflies on nearby flowers at this instant to remind me of the Trinity. You urge me to look at the variegated stones beneath my feet, unsteady to walk on singly, but spread in a multitude making a sturdy path like the community that supports me. You tell me to look all around me and catch the details. See the people who need a touch of You today through me.

2 Timothy 2:224
And the Lord's servant must not be a man of strife: he must be kind to all, ready and able to teach.

April 18

Rest

Dear Jesus,

Sleep beckons, but first my prayer time. I commit my loved ones and myself to You for safekeeping through the night. Then I joyfully present every problem I face for Your providential care.

Next I visualize myself asleep enfolded in Your arms while Your watchful eyes rove about on my behalf. Praise You, Jesus.

What sweet security I enjoy because I trust You totally. Rest comes quickly to my tired body. What a wonderful process.

Psalm 97:10
Let those who love the Lord hate evil, for he guards the lives of His faithful ones and delivers them from the hand of the wicked.

April 19

Kinds of Crosses

Dear Jesus,

I see crosses all around me. Metal crosses with sharp lines, wooden crosses with carved, intricate symbols, porcelain crosses with images. Some are dust collectors on walls whose owners have ceased to see them. Other are ornamental crosses hanging around necks.

Every holy cross serves as a reminder of Your one sacred cross and Your precious life sacrificed - the cross that made kingdom dwellers of people like me. Jesus, You were glorified upon a simple wooden cross.

You've marked me invisibly with Your cross and made me a cross-bearer. My invisible crosses can be carried with dignity and determination. You enable me to have the strength to endure. I carry these daily crosses confident in my ultimate victory over them.

Luke 9:23
Then He said to them all: "Whoever wants to be My disciple must deny themselves and take up their cross daily and follow Me.

April 20

Using Gifts

Dear Jesus,

Great and mighty things I've done by Your grace, as well as small and simple things. Heart-touching things, heart-testing things and heart-blessing things. All done through You.

My God-given gifts were wrapped at the cross and unwrapped on Resurrection day and Pentecost. Mercy, peace and love in abundance were given to be shared with others. May I help transform our present time into a Kingdom-culture.

I long to reflect Your radiance. You and You alone are of ultimate value, Jesus. May I transmit Your message of love as I use my gifts in the world.

1 Corinthians 12:28
And God has placed in the church first of all apostles, second prophets, third teachers, then miracles, then gifts of healing, of helping, of guidance and of different kinds of tongues.

April 21

Authority

Dear Jesus,

In a passage of Scripture evil spirits took over a man and needed to be cast out. The presence of these demons was clearly not acceptable.

I understand this, but have a question. I've often wondered why did the demons inside the man ask to enter the pigs? Did the demons think You would allow them to remain in these animals? And why did you accommodate their request? So that onlookers could see the demons destroyed as the pigs went over the cliff?

For me the most important part of the story Jesus is that you've given me the same authority over demons as Yours. The demons responded instantly to Your command. May I repulse the forces of darkness boldly and without fear through Your Name.

Matthew 8:30-32
So the demons begged Him saying, "If You cast us out, permit us to go away into the herd of swine."

April 22

Critical

Dear Jesus,

Your commands about judging are quite clear. You tell me not to judge at a glance, superficially, by appearance. You say to assess people and situations fairly, and judge cautiously and righteously. And judgment is never about someone's relationship with You, only You determine that Lord.

I'm to encourage, exhort and judge surface behaviors that distance others from You. I must guard myself from developing a critical spirit. You encourage me to be loving always. It's only possible to achieve this with the grace You provide.

John 7:24
Do not judge according to appearance, but judge with righteous judgment.

April 23

Anxiety

Dear Jesus,

At times I feel distressed. My anxiety intensifies as new problems pop up and situations change from bad to worse.

Satan tempts me to discouragement. Then I simply, suddenly, think of You, and a glint of hope glows, then grows within me. I have a Rescuer and a Deliverer. Your help may not be visible instantaneously, but my rescue will happen.

Where does this inclination to trust and peace come from? Of course, from Your Word, Your Grace and Your Spirit. Is this not truly the meaning of being empowered by You?

Psalm 119:32
I run in the path of Your commands for You have set my heart free.

April 24

Ever God

Dear Jesus,

My delight is in You. You're the Instigator of my joy and the Revealer of Goodness. You are the Dispeller of Anger, Destroyer of Anxiety, my Sanctuary-Creator and my Spirit-Lifter!

You're my whatever and however and whenever God. All these "evers" apply because I safely release all control to You. You execute perfect action with perfect timing and demonstrate perfect love every time. No wonder You're my "ever" God!

All these things You are to me, but not only me. You're available to anyone who names You Lord. I love to meditate on all these ways You impact my life now and for-ever.

Deuteronomy 10:17
For the Lord your God is God of gods and Lord of lords, the great God, mighty and awesome, who shows no partiality nor takes a bribe.

April 25

Problems

Dear Jesus,

Words spill out, my thoughts tumble. I try to imagine what lessons You have for me in these present trials. Are there qualities of patience or perseverance You want me to develop?

I recall past experiences of your intervention in my life. In awe I look back upon great good that has come from incidents that seemed dark at first. I'm amazed at the twists and turns of circumstances. Often the good outcomes exceeded my expectation.

Every time I pray, You urge me again to persevere with patience. Every time I ask, I listen and seek my part, Jesus. I do what seems to be the next right thing in each situation. I'm at peace knowing You're with me and always working for my good.

Isaiah 46:4
Even to your old age and gray hairs I am He, I am He who will sustain you. I have made you and I will carry you; I will sustain you and I will rescue.

April 26

Self-delusion

Dear Jesus,

I admit at times I've been prone to selfish motives. Although at the moment I usually didn't recognize self-centeredness in myself. I'd become accustomed to self-serving thoughts, even twisted them so they seemed natural and nice.

My illusions have been punctured by Your Word. Jesus, Your humility and Your authority humbled me. I realized it's You who empower me undeservedly with giftings for divine purposes.

Now I've surrendered self-rulership to Your lordship. I'm privileged to be a servant of Yours, my King, nothing more or less. I removed my self-chosen garment of superiority. I walk free of delusion, embracing fully who You made me to be with all my opportunities and imperfections. May my motives and actions glorify You alone.

Psalm 45:4
And in Your majesty ride prosperously because of truth, humility, and righteousness; and Your right hand shall teach You awesome things.

April 27

One Dot

Dear Jesus,

Life is amazingly short. It seems as if I have but one dot, one spot, one second of life history. In Your Word I read I'm like grass, here today and soon gone. It gives me pause to stop and consider.

I experience one day at a time living out of Your life story for me, Jesus. One dream, one plan and one choice to obey. One me with You. One divine destiny.

One chance to impact my world through You and for You, my Lord. May I use it well.

1 Kings 8:58
...that He may incline our hearts to Himself, to walk in all His ways, and to keep His commandments and His statutes and His judgments, which He commanded our fathers.

April 28

Emptiness

Dear Jesus,

I have friends who dislike any mention of You. Yet they're obviously not happy individuals. I don't know how to guide them to knowledge of You. What possibly can I say to ignite their minds that seem deadened to Your truth?

They scoff at the possibility of a holy virgin birth and devalue Your horrendous crucifixion. They refuse to admit their sinfulness and need for Your exquisite gift of salvation.

Yet I sense an emptiness that seems sad beyond words. Do the heavenlies weep? It comforts me that one day all will know You, Jesus. I only wish it were now. Please guide me to lovingly and wisely be a blessing to these dear people.

Colossians 2:22-23
These things indeed have an appearance of wisdom in self-imposed religion, false humility, and neglect of the body, but are of no value against the indulgence of the flesh.

April 29

Seventy-two

Dear Jesus,

How amazing what seventy-two empowered by You can do! Seventy-two disciples drove out evil spirits and healed the sick with nothing for their journey save a walking stick. No food, no money, no extra clothes, but sandals to be used for dust-shaking in any community that didn't welcome them.

I have more tools to use: church services, Bible studies, Christian books, fellowship groups and retreats. I wonder if these sometimes get in the way of simply doing what the seventy-two did - telling the good news, healing the sick and driving out demons.

Seventy-two were willing to tell the good news about You everywhere, loving people to You wherever they went. Jesus, forgive me when I neglect my holy mission and forget to walk in the shoes of these seventy-two. May I witness in my contemporary world with the confidence and power displayed by these seventy-two.

Luke 10:1
After this the Lord appointed seventy-two others and sent them two by two ahead of Him to every town and place where He was about to go.

April 30

God Who

Dear Jesus,

You're God of Who I Am, God of What I Will Be, and my God Who Opens My World to all possibilities because of Who You Are.

You are my precious Jesus Who holds the dark places of earth together, Who knows the deep places of my heart. God You are Elohim – three Mighty Ones, Father, Son, Holy Spirit. You are the One Who energizes all creation, the One Who energizes me. I praise You, the One Who gives me life and purpose today and forever.

Jesus, I see You everywhere, within me in my energy for doing, urging me to perform well. I sense Your heart charging me with divine love. I look into Your holy eyes and Your compassion becomes mine. Ultimate designer of all that is, You guarantee me a life described as good and a future in Your forever.

Exodus 3:14
And God said to Moses, "I AM WHO I AM." And He said, "Thus you shall say to the children of Israel, 'I AM has sent me to you.'"

May 1

Lasting Love

Dear Jesus,

From the time I was a child, I wanted love and happiness. It took me a long time to figure out where to find it. In the meantime I crammed my life with things, and sought pleasurable experiences, which were always fleeting.

How confusing and empty life seemed at times. How amazing and simple it's become. I've experienced You, my Lord of love who alone bring richness and meaning to all the days of my life.

Knowing You and having You dwelling within me, my Lord of love, I have all the love and happiness I want.

Ps 13:5-6
But I trust in Your unfailing love; my heart rejoices in Your salvation. I will sing the Lord's praise, for He has been good to me.

May 2

Days

Dear Jesus,

Days slide together into seamless strands, sort of like water streaming over a waterfall. Most flow smoothly, easily and apparently inconsequentially. Others are filled with uncertainty, obvious mistakes and chaotic moments. I'd like to snatch those back and yell "Do-over."

Yet I forge forward, knowing all my past days have gone and await Your eternal examination. I treasure every twenty-four hours – savoring the sweetness before tomorrow slips into place.

May I yield moment by moment to Your Holy Spirit's promptings and make each day purposeful. Jesus, I pray my entire life is used well.

Ps 56:13
For You have delivered me from death and my feet from stumbling, that I may walk before God in the light of life.

May 3

Guidance

Dear Jesus,

Guide me please. Help me establish realistic goals for my life. On my own I might make them too high, or conversely not challenge myself enough. You know exactly what my abilities are and what's appropriate for me.

I love it Jesus when You guide me by Your spirit. I appreciate the wise mentors in the flesh that You've placed in my life also to advise me. Human inspiration and affirmation are helpful.

Whatever I accomplish, wherever I go, may You be glorified. I surrender to Your total control over my life.

Psalm 78:72
So He shepherded them according to the integrity of His heart, and guided them by the skillfulness of His hands.

May 4

◆◆◆

Heaven's First Morning

◆◆◆

Dear Jesus,

I like to imagine my first morning in heaven. What will it be like? Will I chat with You and dance through the clouds? May I ride the morning star?

I'd love to climb into Elijah's chariot and see a startled fish emerge from the splitting Red Sea. May I pet the mane of Your white horse and sit among the children You let come close to You?

Heaven's first morning will be so grand! Until then, simply thinking about eternity enthralls me.

Exodus 15:13
In Your unfailing love You will lead the people you have redeemed. In Your strength You will guide them to Your holy dwelling.

May 5

Conversation With God

Dear Jesus,

You've told me not to let anyone tell me it's unusual for You to talk to any person who will listen. Why would You not converse with each person You love? Don't humans speak to those they love?

I know You speak to my heart. Jesus, I delight in our intimate conversations. You also speak through creation. And I read Scripture for more messages from You. Your precious words are recorded for all to see.

Jesus, You speak one on one to waiting hearts daily who need only take the time to be still and listen. What a privilege to hear You.

1 Sam 3:10
Now the Lord came and stood and called as at other times, "Samuel! Samuel!" And Samuel answered, "Speak, for Your servant hears."

May 6

Eighteen Years

Dear Jesus,

For eighteen years a precious woman mentioned in the Bible by Luke was stooped, bent completely forward, unable to look. Lord, You said a demon of sickness had deformed her. Then miraculously You made her right.

Demons are real. They flee when ordered out by Your authority.

Jesus, lay Your hands on me as well. May I always look to You, not bent by emotions or demons. May I walk tall and strong, made straight by Your hand and kept strong by Your power.

Luke 13:10-13
Now He was teaching in one of the synagogues on the Sabbath. And behold, there was a woman who had a spirit of infirmity eighteen years, and was bent over and could in no way raise herself up. But when Jesus saw her, He called her to Him and said to her, "Woman, you are loosed from your infirmity." And He laid His hands on her, and immediately she was made straight, and glorified God.

Those Moments

Dear Jesus,

Jesus, those moments when I'm low, when sickness comes out of nowhere and fills me with fear, I need you near. You flood me with hope and wholeness. Your healing touch restores me.

Jesus, those moments when insecurity pops up and fills me with doubt, I need You near. You flood me with confidence and my joy again begins to flow.

Jesus, I can never describe adequately what it means to me to know that You're always with me, whatever happens wherever I go.

Psalm 73:25-26
Whom have I in heaven but You? And earth has nothing I desire besides You. My flesh and my heart may fail, but God is the strength of my heart and my portion forever.

May 8

Night Thoughts

Dear Jesus,

In the middle of the night when we're all alone, nobody but us Jesus, I sense Your presence and feel Your glow all around me. I sense Your shield, favor and fire. Your shield guards me, Your favor blesses me and Your fire ignites my spirit.

In loving You, I'm completely fulfilled, and totally, authentically me. You create substance for my hope, You instill sparks of faith in me and inspire charity within my heart.

Jesus, my voice is filled with praise. Peace reigns within my world.

Psalm 63:6,7
On my bed I remember You; I think of You through the watches of the night.

May 9

The Word

Dear Jesus,

I sense Your presence through reading Scripture. Your Word of Truth holds power. It's my Lifestyle-Changer, Mountain-Mover, Difference-Maker, Wisdom-Source and Encouragement-Fountain.

Daily I open Your Word, my God Book, to absorb Your Biblical principles and receive Your counsel. I like finding the treasures in Your Word. I treasure the purity and integrity I read about. I want to live according to Biblical principles in holiness honoring You.

Make me wise and strong by Your Word. And keep me forever strong by these frequent times with You in Your Word. Jesus, I treasure them. Charge me up and set me loose in the world to teach Your Word.

Psalm 119:15-16
I meditate on Your precepts and consider Your ways. I delight in Your decrees; I will not neglect Your word.

May 10

Moving Temples

Dear Jesus,

People sit in pretty pews or on soft, upholstered chairs, and visit with one other at church suppers or weekly prayer meetings. Pastors send flyers to the community inviting people to visit. Come into church, be a regular attendee and tithe. Isn't church swell? There's nothing wrong with this, but God, You're not confined by walls.

You're best proclaimed from mountaintops and displayed by love and joy in our daily lives. You're not a building or a program. You've made us moving temples - our torches are a life-giving message.

We were created to display real words of truth and deeds of love wherever we are. And so, may I.

2 Cor. 6:16s
What agreement is there between the temple of God and idols? For we are the temple of the living God. As God has said: "I will live with them and walk among them, and I will be their God, and they will be my people."

May 11

The Presence

Dear Jesus,

The aura of Your presence when You appeared on earth had to be overwhelming. I can easily understand why the apostle John fell into a trance when you appeared to him.

How can human senses absorb Your supernatural essence? The very thought of You thrills me! In Your physical presence I'd surely swoon.

Jesus, I yearn for the moment when I'm overcome by Your glory as I see You face to face. Only an eternity in Your presence will be enough for me.

Exodus 15:11
Who among the gods is like You, Lord? Who is like You—majestic in holiness, awesome in glory, working wonders?

May 12

Messenger

Dear Jesus,

I know that You are real and true. I once had doubts, but no longer since I sought and found the truth about You. I'm sad many do not know You. Jesus, make me a messenger with the ability to teach others to comprehend Your truth.

This world needs You.

May my love speak even louder than the words I use. Fully empower me by Your Spirit. Give me authority, boldness and a strong anointing to proclaim Your reality to others.

Haggai 1:13
Then Haggai, the Lord's messenger, gave this message of the Lord to the people: "I am with you," declares the Lord.

Creation

Dear Jesus,

Your process of creation fascinates me. When darkness covered a formless earth You chose to make it bright. You knew light would be good. Was it always Your plan to separate day from night? What did You first see when You called dry land forth from the expanse of waters under the heavens? When You collected water for the seas, You must have been pleased for You stopped to give Your approval.

I would have liked to be there when birds and fish were spoken into existence and blessed with the ability to multiply. How delightful to watch animals strut forth fit and varied even before the creation of male and female made in Your image!

The lushness of vegetation yielding seed came next. Jesus, You declared Your infinite variety good. You give me continual reminders of providential care, like the sun and moon to mark seasons, days and years. How intricate, precise and awesome Your creation is!

Genesis 1:1

In the beginning God created the heavens and the earth. The earth was without form, and void; and darkness was on the face of the deep. And the Spirit of God was hovering over the face of the waters.

Spirals

Dear Jesus,

My choices in life are similar to two spiral staircases – one leads up and one down - stubbornness and stupidity or humility and wisdom. My way or Your way.

I dabble with danger when I ignore signs of Your displeasure from my transgressions. Life on the edge is dangerous. A little evil leads to more until my heart no longer beats with divine purpose. To sin is to live in bondage and deception. Then Satan taunts me that rescue is hopeless. Liar!

Life in, through, and with You is smooth and free. Jesus, I choose to spiral up, make wholesome choices, and wisely obey Your laws. It's tough at times – gossip is tempting, flirting seems innocent at first and a lie is often easier in the moment. Jesus, I choose the upward spiral of obedience and holiness that pleases You.

Deuteronomy 30:19
This day I call the heavens and the earth as witnesses against you that I have set before you life and death, blessings and curses. Now choose life, so that you and your children may live.

Names

Dear Jesus,

How awesome it must have been for some individuals in Scripture to have their names announced before birth by God. What an honor for Isaac, Solomon, Josiah and John the Baptist!

I'm content to have my name merely known by You, Jesus. What joy to be adopted into Your kingly bloodline.

I eagerly await the day when I hear my name spoken aloud by You. Humbly I hope You will add "good and faithful."

Psalm 105:3
Glory in His holy name; let the hearts of those who seek the Lord rejoice.

Isaac

Dear Jesus,

Isaac's elderly mother-to-be Sarai laughed when she was informed of Issac's approaching birth. She was admonished for her lack of faith. Laughter at the right time is a gift. At the wrong time it can be a curse.

Unfortunately, her laughing signified doubting God, as Sarai discovered. After Issac's birth Sarai spoke her son's name over and over with delight all the rest of her life. She learned that belief always brings blessings.

How like You Jesus to turn her error into joy when finally she trusted. Because of my confidence in You, I can laugh also. I laugh when fear springs up about my future. I trust You during trials. You bless me with glorious joy!

Genesis 21:2, 3, 6, 7
Sarah became pregnant and bore a son to Abraham in his old age, at the very time God had promised him.

May 17

Priorities

Dear Jesus,

You assure me I can have confidence in Your perfect ways. Divine Listener, You hear my heart like no human can. You have deep understanding and perfect knowledge of my motives.

Sometimes guilt suppresses my spirit and sends shame seething within me. It sickens my soul. Regret rises up and cries out. I'm seared and scorched. But I repent and You clean me right up, Lord. You're the Designer of my mouth, ears and searcher of my heart. You cleanse me completely and I no longer feel shame.

You help me keep my actions and priorities right. I live to serve You always and obey Your perfect will.

Ezekiel 21: 26-27
This is what the Sovereign Lord says: "Take off the turban, remove the crown. It will not be as it was: The lowly will be exalted and the exalted will be brought low. A ruin! A ruin! I will make it a ruin! The crown will not be restored until He to whom it rightfully belongs shall come; to Him I will give it."

May 18

Wisdom

Dear Jesus,

In the Old Testament I read about a time long ago when the Queen of Sheba visited Solomon. She'd heard of his great wisdom and wished to experience it for herself. She knew wisdom was far more important than wealth.

Jesus, I too daily seek Your wisdom that's kept sacred and preserved in Scripture and tradition. I need Your holy insights and inspiration. A dry well cannot give water, nor can an ignorant mind produce knowledge. I use thinking and reflection as my common daily tools.

Parents and grandparents guide children of future generations with inflow and outflow of their knowledge about You and Your ways. This ensures the transfer of spiritual knowledge to the future. May they always seek wisdom from You and teach it to their young.

Psalm 49:3-5
My mouth will speak words of wisdom; the meditation of my heart will give you understanding. I will turn my ear to a proverb; with the harp I will expound my riddle: Why should I fear when evil days come, when wicked deceivers surround me—

May 19

Intrigued

Dear Jesus,

Your Word intrigues me. Within Scripture I read about things I've never heard of like red sandalwood brought from Ophir and almugwood, a sweet-smelling tree, with strong wood. Almugwood was used to make supports for Your temple, yet was pliable enough to form harps and lyres for the musicians.

Jesus, Your world, all Your creation, never ceases to amaze me. How many lifetimes would I have to live to experience all You've made?

Oh the richness, the variety, the complexity and the simplicity of Your truth, Your work and Your world.

2 Chronicles 9:10,11
Also, the servants of Hiram and the servants of Solomon, who brought gold from Ophir, brought almugwood and precious stones. And the king made walkways of the almugwood for the house of the Lord and for the king's house, also harps and stringed instruments for singers; and there were none such as these seen before in the land of Judah.

Demons

Dear Jesus,

We seldom hear warnings nowadays about demonic activity. How surprising since demons still roam the earth. People often don't know that it's demonic forces bringing them low.

Times were different, Jesus, when You lived among us. Most people knew demons were real and talked about them freely. They understood demons' power to torture and destroy.

Jesus, You equip me with strength and ability to fight demonic forces just as You equipped the seventy-two disciples You sent forth to fight demon battles. You promise that no demon can harm me. May I use Your power to free others captured by demonic wiles. May only Your power prevail.

1 Timothy 4:1-2
The Spirit clearly says that in later times some will abandon the faith and follow deceiving spirits and things taught by demons. Such teachings come through hypocritical liars, whose consciences have been seared as with a hot iron.

May 21

Salt

Dear Jesus,

What an interesting image. You say I should be like salt. I don't want to be weak salt, flat salt, tasteless salt or fit-for-nothing salt.

Instead I yearn to be strong salt, preserving salt and heaven-flavored salt. I want to help people spice up their lives and add to their savor as only salt can do.

Jesus, may I be super-salty for Thee.

Matthew 5:13
You are the salt of the earth. But if the salt loses its saltiness, how can it be made salty again? It is no longer good for anything, except to be thrown out and trampled underfoot.

May 22

Sheep Hunt

Dear Jesus,

Some dear people I know have lost their way through life. My words aren't getting through to them. They refuse to hear Your truth. What a waste of Kingdom potential! All my efforts have been as nothing, Jesus.

Go after them please. I'm on my knees praying they can be reached. These people are such a treasure - I love them beyond measure and can't bear for them to be lost. Shepherd them to safety please. Use Your staff if You must, do whatever it takes.

If You want to use me to rescue them, guide me to know the best way. May these dear people be in heaven some day.

Ezekiel 34:11
For thus says the Lord God: "Indeed I Myself will search for My sheep and seek them out."

May 23

Healing Faith

Dear Jesus,

Many people need a touch of divine healing. I see their pain. I know I'm unworthy to be an instrument of healing, yet I'm eager to pray and fast for people's healings.

To my amazement, Jesus, You say You know I'm not worthy, but my worthiness isn't an issue. Having faith in You is all it takes, simple faith in Your supernatural power. You've made healing available for all. Only trust and believe You say and leave outcomes to You. Some individuals will be visibly healed now, but all will be healed some day, whether on earth or in heaven.

You remind me that a healthy soul takes priority over bodily health. Help me be faith-filled and diligent to pray daily for physical, emotional and spiritual healings for all the sick I encounter.

Luke 8:47-48
Now when the woman saw that she was not hidden, she came trembling; and falling down before Him, she declared to Him in the presence of all the people the reason she had touched Him and how she was healed immediately. And He said to her, "Daughter, be of good cheer; your faith has made you well. Go in peace."

Everything

Dear Jesus,

Your Gospel teaches that surrendering ownership over every possession isn't necessary, but surrendering lordship over them is essential! All things belong to You Lord. What matters is having my priorities right.

Some individuals may hesitate to choose Your lordship, but not me, not for a second. What an easy decision. Lord, I choose the only treasure worth keeping– knowing, loving and serving You. Keep me worthy Jesus to receive all the blessings You promise.

You are more valuable than any earthly possession.

Matthew 19:21
Jesus said to him, "If you want to be perfect, go, sell what you have and give to the poor, and you will have treasure in heaven; and come, follow Me."

May 25

The Judge

Dear Jesus,

You told the story of the persistent widow who annoyed the judge when she sought justice and protection. She wouldn't stop badgering him for help.

This widow upset the unjust judge because he realized she wouldn't quit until her need was satisfied. Finally he responded to her plea.

Jesus, You're my great and just judge and my persistent asking doesn't annoy, but pleases You. I appreciate that You're always available and willing to help me. I'm forever grateful for answers to my prayers.

Luke 18:2-8
There was in a certain city a judge who did not fear God nor regard man. Now there was a widow in that city; and she came to him, saying, get justice for me from my adversary. And he would not for a while; but afterward he said within himself, Though I do not fear God nor regard man, yet because this widow troubles me I will avenge her, lest by her continual coming she weary me.

May 26

Mystery

Dear Jesus,

The people walked next to You, Living Truth, yet comprehended You not. As the Living Word of God, You were flogged and killed, and then mysteriously arose from the dead.

The closed minds of people probably saddened You more than their jeers and spit. Your only intention was relieving human anguish and releasing their souls from bondage. You desired only good for them.

A few souls abandoned their fears and misconceptions and ventured near to You. Yet many people never knew the fullness of Your truth. To them You remained a distant phenomenon. Not so for me. I'll proclaim it everywhere: You are my Lord and my God.

Psalm 33:18
Behold, the eye of the Lord is on those who fear Him, on those who hope in His mercy.

Death

Dear Jesus,

Death comes swiftly and unexpectantly. I received news today about a family member who is now in Your presence. Life's problems and difficult challenges are over for this dear one.

Our sadness is acute. We liked knowing this person walked and lived among us. That's not to say we would ever want to hold him back from becoming a heaven-dweller, only that we'd have preferred not quite yet.

May his passing help us treasure one another even more during the short time we exist together in this world.

2 Corinthians 5:1-5
For we know that if our temporary, earthly dwelling is destroyed, we have a building from God, an eternal dwelling in the heavens, not made with hands. Indeed, we groan in this body, desiring to put on our dwelling from heaven, since, when we are clothed, we will not be found naked. Indeed, we groan while we are in this tent, burdened as we are, because we do not want to be unclothed but clothed, so that mortality may be swallowed up by life.

May 28

Scary Words

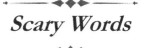

Dear Jesus,

The words "Thy Kingdom come!" might sound scary to those who don't know You. When You return to earth, Jesus, anything covered up or hidden will be revealed. Things done in the dark will be seen. Words spoken in privacy will be heard and whispers will be loudly proclaimed.

There's no need to dread this time, Jesus, You say. We need only fear the one who can hurl humans into hell. If we declare on earth before men that we know and worship You, we'll be acknowledged in the presence of God and the angels! How awesome!

Jesus, what sweet words are these!

Psalm 84:11
For the Lord God is a sun and shield; The Lord will give grace and glory; No good thing will He withhold from those who walk uprightly.

May 29

Mind's Eye

Dear Jesus,

I see You, Jesus, in my mind's eye in Samaria at the well. I picture You in the Temple tossing out the greedy men. I visualize You in the desert thwarting Satan. I hear You in the boat speaking calm into the storm.

I hold these images in my mind. All the while You are Father-led, Spirit-willed, and heavenly focused. Always You knew that You were walking toward Gethsemane. Jesus, wherever You were, You acted on my behalf to bless me.

One day You, who once rode a lowly colt, will ride the white horse of Revelation. I can hardly wait to see this.

John 10:28-30
And I give them eternal life, and they shall never perish; neither shall anyone snatch them out of My hand. My Father, who has given them to Me, is greater than all; and no one is able to snatch them out of My Father's hand. I and My Father are one."

May 30

Lessons

Dear Jesus,

Your disciples thought they had a great idea. They wanted You to command fire to come down upon your enemies. "Destroy those who refuse to accept You," they suggested. This sounded like a good method to many.

But Your plan was to save people from the penalty of death and free them from the distress of sin, not to punish or hurt unbelievers.

Mercy and grace is what You insist on for all. Your disciples had much to learn. Jesus, so do I.

Psalm 25:4
Show me Your ways, O Lord; Teach me Your paths.

May 31

Signs

Dear Jesus,

How fortunate the Israelites were to have visible signs of Your presence Lord! Fire and a cloud!

You give me signs through reading about Scriptural events that are deep with meaning and full of power. These signs were given for my instruction:
The sign of the Israelites teaches me that rebellion leads to disaster.
The sign of Jonah teaches me that disobedience cannot be tolerated.
The sign of Mary teaches me that holiness leads to honor.
The sign of the Pharisees teaches me that pride leads to false belief.
The sign of Jesus teaches me that Your cross leads to life.
The signs of the Holy Spirit teach me that miracles still abound.
Jesus, Your signs in Scripture teach me and inspire me.

Psalm 86:17
Show me a sign for good, that those who hate me may see it and be ashamed, because You, Lord, have helped me and comforted me.

June 1

Seed

Dear Jesus,

It's Your Seed – the truth contained in Your Word - that holds the power to transform lives.

Your Gospel teaches that seed falls on different kinds of ground: good soil, thorn-covered and rocky. Some seed holds fast in the ground and will yield a crop of fruit. Other seed is choked by thorns and withers away. Still other seed is smashed by walkers and eaten by birds - what a waste.

Jesus, water and light are required for seed to grow. Spending time in prayer, study of the Word and Christian fellowship supplies the necessary nutrients for my soil. I can't control the "soil" of others, but I can be vigilant about my own. I await Your harvest in due season.

2 Corinthians 9:10-11
Now may He who supplies seed to the sower, and bread for food, supply and multiply the seed you have sown and increase the fruits of your righteousness, while you are enriched in everything for all liberality, which causes thanksgiving through us to God.

June 2

Teacher

Dear Jesus,

You're my spiritual director and my personal teacher. Your Word filled with stories and examples gives me abundant lessons. Holy Spirit, source of divine wisdom and counsel, I depend upon Your discernment to absorb what I need for my circumstances.

You transmit both heart knowledge and head knowledge to me and to anyone who desires to learn. And You give me the Holy Spirit nudges I need for applying Your principles to my life.

What a great teacher You are. I'm blessed beyond words and forever grateful to be Your student.

Psalm 86:10-11
For You are great, and do wondrous things; You alone are God. Teach me Your way, O Lord; I will walk in Your truth; unite my heart to fear Your name.

June 3

Fullness

Dear Jesus,

How could someone literally see You, experience Your blessings, hear Your voice and still not believe?

How is it possible that people who walked at your side were able to deny the reality of Your love and power? Can the shield of self-absorption be so strong that it's not penetrated by the very presence of God?

How extraordinary because You placed spiritual desire in every heart. An emptiness and yearning for "something more" longs to be filled. There are ways to try to fill this need with frivolous experiences and material things. They don't work. I know. I've tried. How grateful I am to finally know You and the fullness of life with You.

Ephesians 1:13-14
In Him [Christ] you also trusted, after you heard the word of truth, the gospel of your salvation; in whom also, having believed, you were sealed with the Holy Spirit of promise, who is the guarantee of our inheritance until the redemption of the purchased possession, to the praise of His glory.

June 4

Mini-miracles

Dear Jesus,

I see mini-miracles every day. I'm amazed at the flight of birds. Squirrel and chipmunks abuzz with chatter and movement fascinate me. The extraordinary skies you create are more exquisite than a Monet painting. Mini-miracles abound.

I see major miracles, too. Sometimes You allow me to witness human "I forgive's" and "I'm sorry's." Dead souls revitalized with life are real, present-day miracles. New paths to be braved with courage because people can do "all things through Christ who strengthens them." These are amazing acts of God.

Miracle-making Father, Jesus and Holy Spirit, You astound me daily!

Psalm 148:113
Let them praise the name of the Lord, for His name alone is exalted; His splendor is above the earth and the heavens.

June 5

Life

Dear Jesus,

You are the source and end purpose of everything. You are the funnel and the filter of all things. Life is all about You, in You, through You and for You.

It's easy to momentarily forget this important reality as the world pulls me. Of course, You want me to enjoy the wholesome life experiences available to me.

Always I need to recognize that all that's good in life comes from You, exists through You and moves toward completion in You, Jesus. May I be mindful of this every day!

Psalm 62:4
Surely they intend to topple me from my lofty place; they take delight in lies. With their mouths they bless, but in their hearts they curse.

June 6

Spiritual Might

Dear Jesus,

Morning and a new day begins. Streaks of brightness filter through my blinds. An awesome interplay of light, mixed with shadows, creates beauty and makes me ponder the role of darkness. Is it to emphasize the beautiful and bright?

I'm fresh and sin-free when I awake. Jesus, I wish temptations didn't exist, sin had no power and Satan didn't try so hard to make me falter. Which brings up a perplexing question. Why let evil exist? You permit Satan to prowl about seeking whomever he can entice into evil. Perhaps his existence makes my resolve to remain connected with You stronger.

You've given me spiritual might to strengthen me in fighting evil and doing right. Both light and darkness interplay within me testing my personality and character. Jesus, You've taught me I'm always free to choose how I respond. When evening of today comes, may I still be beautiful and sin free. My desire is only to please You.

Psalm 37:27-28
Depart from evil, and do good; and dwell forevermore. For the Lord loves justice, and does not forsake His saints; they are preserved forever, but the descendants of the wicked shall be cut off.

June 7

Sabbath

Dear Jesus,

You tell me observing the Sabbath is a privilege. You insist I guard this day of seven and use it as a time of refreshment. Keep the day holy. No work by God's order! A true Sabbath of rest - an entire day without work. A holy call to do nothing at all!

Amazingly, the Sabbath is designed to bless me. Jesus, how thoughtful and kind of You to insist that I take a day off. You've made honoring the Sabbath a statute forever, to be observed in every generation and within every nation. I long to comply but can I? Most people need to work non-stop to get ahead or at least keep up. Won't I fall behind if I give up my Sabbath work?

You assure me You'll provide. I choose to trust You. Because You command it, I've determined to honor the Sabbath.

Isaiah 58:13-14

If you keep your feet from breaking the Sabbath and from doing as you please on my holy day, if you call the Sabbath a delight and the Lord's holy day honorable, and if you honor it by not going your own way and not doing as you please or speaking idle words, then you will find your joy in the Lord.

Span of Life

Dear Jesus,

The span of each person's life is a mystery. How long shall it be? How many years have You designated for my body to experience earthly life?

For some the span of life seems, in human opinion, lengthy, for others too short. I'm glad You're in charge, Jesus, of defining years and giving occasional extensions, like the fifteen years faithful Hezekiah received. Then again, sometimes You cut a life short like with haughty Herod.

Jesus, however many years you've determined for me I'll treasure each one. I'll use each day as a collection of moments to be lived well. I embrace both the challenges and pleasures of living fully the adventure of my one amazing life.

Psalm 39:4-5
Show me, Lord, my life's end and the number of my days; let me know how fleeting my life is. You have made my days a mere handbreadth; the span of my years is as nothing before You. Everyone is but a breath, even those who seem secure.

June 9

Temple

Dear Jesus,

How appalling when Your sacred temple was turned into a hangout for buying and selling. Your house of holiness for all the nations was transformed into a roost for robbers! The temple enclosure was actually made into a traffic short cut.

How rightfully angry You were! The multitude was struck with astonishment at your reaction. You drove forth the desecrators and instilled fear in the chief priests who had allowed these violations.

Jesus, how painful it had to be to see your Father's house in this state. I also guard a holy temple. May I keep sacred my physical body, the Holy Spirit's dwelling place. I long to remain pure of defilement. May my body, my temple, be forever fit for Your presence.

1 Corinthians 3:16, 17
Don't you know that you yourselves are God's temple and that God's Spirit dwells in your midst? If anyone destroys God's temple, God will destroy that person; for God's temple is sacred, and you together are that temple.

June 10

Royalty

Dear Jesus,

The table is set. They're about to arrive - these sons and daughters You've given me to teach and guide.

I've called them from their play and chores. Your princes and princesses shall dine at my side. Help me remember each meal is a sacred time, an interlude for training and loving. Jesus, they're imperfect in their natural state, but eager and willing to learn. These little lords and ladies are the royalty You've sent into our home and entrusted to me.

May I be mindful of their ages and abilities and tender and wise. Certainly parenting is the greatest work I can do. It's a mighty responsibility. No role is holier. You've made me a model my children are ready to follow. Help me, Lord. These royal youth must be raised to honor You, my King.

1 Peter 2:9-10
But you are a chosen people, a royal priesthood, a holy nation, God's special possession, that you may declare the praises of him who called you out of darkness into His wonderful light. Once you were not a people, but now you are the people of God; once you had not received mercy, but now you have received mercy.

June 11

Two Sons

Dear Jesus,

I ponder the story You told of two sons. A seemingly "good" son and a "bad" son. A steady son, and a wandering son. One content soul, one restless heart. Lovers of life and joy both.

The "good" son was respectful but became bitter, the other was wild and unappreciative. One day, the rebellious son learned a lesson through squandering his inheritance and living in harsh deprivation. He remembered the warm security of his former home and longed to return. The "good" son resented his brother's coming home and getting his position of sonship restored.

Seemingly "good" son, "bad" son, both teach me powerful lessons. Two sons equally loved, needed to learn to appreciate their father, express gratitude and celebrate life. May I be mindful to do the same.

Luke 15:22-24

But the father said to his servants, "Quick! Bring the best robe and put it on him. Put a ring on his finger and sandals on his feet. Bring the fattened calf and kill it. Let's have a feast and celebrate. For this son of mine was dead and is alive again; he was lost and is found." So they began to celebrate.

June 12

Pharisees

Dear Jesus,

The Pharisees studied You as they stalked You. They sifted Your words. Their twisted tongues unleashed questions to trap You. These self-seekers didn't know what to make of Your selfless love. Perfection of God, You became man's prey.

Satan played these religious leaders well. They conspired to catch You with their evil words. Darkness and deceit couldn't hold You Jesus. In three days the Spirit set You free. Your empty tomb revealed undeniable truth - fully God, You walked earth again for all to see.

Generation after generation has passed. You who the Pharisees wanted to destroy, the humble Son of God, live on in the hearts of Your followers. Evil could not stop Your message of love, Jesus, my Lord and God.

Matthew 23:27-28
Woe to you, teachers of the law and Pharisees, you hypocrites! You are like whitewashed tombs, which look beautiful on the outside but on the inside are full of the bones of the dead and everything unclean. In the same way, on the outside you appear to people as righteous but on the inside you are full of hypocrisy and wickedness.

June 13

Kingdom

Dear Jesus,

I think, finally, I understand. Thy kingdom come means my kingdom must go. Your way Jesus means not choosing my own path however desirable. These other paths may well end up being fruitless.

Thy will, Jesus, means my ego cannot reign. When I cease endless striving I can live a truly happy stress-free life.

Jesus, it's so simple. Why do I struggle? Seeking Your kingdom and Your way is best.

Matthew 13:11-12

He [Jesus] replied, Because the knowledge of the secrets of the kingdom of heaven has been given to you, but not to them. Whoever has will be given more, and they will have an abundance. Whoever does not have, even what they have will be taken from them.

June 14

Authority

Dear Jesus,

While upon this earth You called Yourself -
A fire starter,
A division-maker.
A unity-restorer.
A peace-giver,
A peace-breaker,
A rule-changer.
A new priority-maker,
A kingdom-creator.

These heavy tasks required a mighty hand and a holy heart. Such works were fit for one alone – the amazing, beloved, only Son of God.

Now Jesus, You've made some of these tasks mine as well and empowered me with Your Holy Spirit to succeed. How amazing!

Psalm 145:3
Great is the Lord and most worthy of praise; His greatness no one can fathom.

June 15

◆◆◆

Mount of Olives

◆◆◆

Dear Jesus,

Many nights at the mount called Olives, prior to the fateful night of Your betrayal, were quiet times of rest after teaching in the temple courts. But some were evenings of turmoil, too, because You spoke of what lay ahead, Your soon-coming agony.

It had to be hard to think of anything else, yet Jesus You did as You taught Your followers. You prepared the way for me at this holy place called Olives through the plans soon to be recorded in the four gospels.

Jesus, I too have lessons to learn when I'm on my own Mount Olives of agony. Life is extremely hard at times. Only my faith in You gives me the strength to carry on.

Psalm 145:13b, 14
The Lord is trustworthy in all He promises and faithful in all He does. The Lord upholds all who fall and lifts up all who are bowed down.

June 16

Apparel

Dear Jesus,

You've issued me an invitation to heaven, to everlasting, sacred joy!

Jesus, I accept! However, I don't have the right apparel. The garment of fear I've worn clings, the garment of self-pity has nearly destroyed me and I want to rip off this garment of insecurity. Wait. I shall slip into the glowing garment of holiness You've provided. I once thought I'd never be dressed appropriately, but Lord You provide my perfect wardrobe.

What gifts shall I bring? Nothing tangible You say. Only invisible gifts like trust and obedience. Oh Jesus, gracious Host, I can surely bring these. Let the celebration begin!

Psalm 73:27, 28
Those who are far from You will perish; You destroy all who are unfaithful to You. But as for me, it is good to be near God. I have made the Sovereign Lord my refuge; I will tell of all Your deeds.

June 17

Temptation

Dear Jesus,

The key to conquest over sin has been recorded for all generations and made clear in the Lord's Prayer. A simple, powerful command- pray that you may not enter into temptation. And also within the prayer, deliver me from evil.

Jesus, overcoming temptation is clearly my desire. The secret to succeed over sin is stated in the Our Father. But often I slip into making this more difficult, flirting with bitterness and find myself failing to act as I should.

Jesus, help me resist every semblance of the evil I could easily engage in. Victory over sin can be mine.

Revelation 3:8
I know your deeds. See, I have placed before you an open door that no one can shut. I know that you have little strength, yet you have kept My word and have not denied My name.

June 18

Fullness of Joy

Dear Jesus,

Today and every day You say, "I will be your God, I will be your life. Celebrate and rejoice, again I say rejoice."

Dear Jesus can this be true? A life of constant joy is pleasing to You? You want me to laugh and abandon myself to joy? May I? What about cross-carrying and fasting?

These too have a place You say, but never were meant to take away your deep joy. Jesus, laughter floods my heart! How awesome that You would allow such delight! The fullness of joy begins on earth indeed! Hallelujah!

Psalm 108:1b
My heart, O God, is steadfast; I will sing and make music with all my soul.

June 19

Cup

Dear Jesus,

An angel from heaven strengthened Your Spirit at a low point of Your life on earth. Often, I too become weak. Jesus, I'd appreciate it if You'd send an angel my way now and then. My cup is not of death, yet at times quite difficult all the same.

Jesus, You set an example for me when You experienced agony on earth. Intently and earnestly You prayed and asked for Your cup of suffering to be removed. Yet always You sought not Your will, but Abba's, Your Father's.

Jesus I pray You'll help me be strong enough to drink from the cup set before me.

Romans 8:34-37
Who then is the one who condemns? No one. Christ Jesus who died—more than that, who was raised to life—is at the right hand of God and is also interceding for us. Who shall separate us from the love of Christ? Shall trouble or hardship or persecution or famine or nakedness or danger or sword?...No, in all these things we are more than conquerors through Him who loved us.

June 20

Perfection

Dear Jesus,

You never do too little. You never act too late. Everything You do is perfect. Your perfection in nature is evident all around me.

Jesus, I am grossly unworthy, yet You perfect me and create beauty within my imperfect life.

I never thought the word perfect could in any way be associated with me. Jesus, I rejoice that You keep Your promise to perfect not just me, but all that concerns me.

Deuteronomy 32:4
He is the Rock, His works are perfect, and all His ways are just. A faithful God who does no wrong, upright and just is He.

June 21

Watchfulness

Dear Jesus,

Because their minds and hearts were dull, the apostles failed to understand the meaning of events like Your miraculous dinner for thousands. Constant and abundant provision? How could it be? When You walked on that raging sea to reach them, the apostles were astonished. Miracle-Working Son of God? Jesus, how could they be so dense?

Then again, Jesus, how can I be? Why do I so soon forget that Your care for me is constant? Even during my busy, crazy days Your watchfulness over me never ceases. You respond to my every need. And when unpleasant outcomes occur, You turn them into an ultimate plan for good.

Why? Because of Your immense love operating through Your miracle-working power. What a combination!

Psalm 73:23b, 24
Nevertheless I [the Lord] am continually with You; You hold me by my right hand.

June 22

Extravagance

Dear Jesus,

Dinner leftovers were fine by You, even twelve baskets full. You always produce enough, and often bless with more.

You are an extravagant God, giver beyond measure. The fruit of the fields are more than birds can eat, and the blessings I experience are more than I can fathom.

Giver extraordinaire, may I be generous with Your same measure. Open my fist that sometimes clings too tightly so I may model Your extravagance always.

John 6:12-13
So when they were filled, He said to His disciples, "Gather up the fragments that remain, so that nothing is lost." Therefore they gathered them up, and filled twelve baskets with the fragments of the five barley loaves, which were left over by those who had eaten.

June 23

Release

Dear Jesus,

Persistent pain signals distress and insistently demands my attention, whether the problem is physical or spiritual. It's horrid to endure physical discomfort or spiritual agony. How pain hurts! How deeply I long for relief and freedom!

Nerve-ending physical fire, spiritual twinges of conscience or stabs of guilt. Gut-wrenching pain. Systems alert, do something, relieve the body and heal the soul. At such times freedom from pain is the only desire. Jesus, may I heed the signals, endure the travail as long as necessary and read the message pain tells. And then be free of it.

I praise You for showing me how to be released from the clutches of debilitating pain. I long to remain in physical and spiritual health and holiness.

Romans 5:3-5
Not only so, but we also glory in our sufferings, because we know that suffering produces perseverance; perseverance, character; and character, hope. And hope does not put us to shame, because God's love has been poured out into our hearts through the Holy Spirit, who has been given to us.

June 24

Opinion

Dear Jesus,

The opinion of others used to matter a lot to me. I admit to being an approval-seeker. Since understanding the sacrifice of Your death for me upon Calvary's cross, I consider Your opinion alone.

I can live without concern over condemnation because Lord, You quickly examine and acquit me. You know my aims, reveal my motives and You forgive my sins.

I trust Your judgment about me completely. You formed me, You know when I sit or stand. With all due respect, human opinion means nothing. Only Your assessment matters. Jesus, what a gift to be free!

Psalm 56:4,5
In God, whose word I praise—in God I trust and am not afraid. What can mere mortals do to me?

June 25

Commander-in-Chief

Dear Jesus,

What an awesome commander-in-chief and great war strategist You are. In the Old Testament You used simple weapons for battle like empty pitchers with torches inside. You ordered trumpet sounds to destroy fortifications and brought Your people to victory. You defeated an army with a parted sea.

Jesus, I'm honored to be your soldier, ready for combat. No battle is too great for me after You train me. I await your orders and Your incredible power working through me to accomplish Your purposes. Let the world around me fall apart. I will not fear.

Your promises are incredible Lord. Inner security is mine when I am clothed in Your armor. Nothing can touch me because I dwell with You. People may scream and deride me. I need only follow You, my divine commander-in-chief.

Deuteronomy 11:26-28
See, I am setting before you today a blessing and a curse—the blessing if you obey the commands of the Lord your God that I am giving you today; the curse if you disobey the commands of the Lord your God and turn from the way that I command you today...

June 26

Power-Giver

Dear Jesus,

I'm grateful that You've implanted spiritual strength in me and given me authority over the power of any enemy - this world, my flesh or the devil. I need only use the spiritual weapons that You've made available for me - the sword of the Spirit, the powerful Word of God.

No spiritual battle will be lost. You're my Power-Giver. In You victory is assured. I'm able to identify some enemies easily, others are subtler. No matter, I will defeat them all. Nothing external or internal can defeat me - no selfishness, no serpent, no condemnation.

The enemy can't be victorious over me when I rely on You. How awesome!

2 Samuel 22:36-37
You make your saving help my shield; Your help has made me great. You provide a broad path for my feet, so that my ankles do not give way.

June 27

Hiding Places

Dear Jesus,

Emotional and spiritual hiding places exist everywhere: isolation, busyness, depression and anger. I've used some of them. Withdrawal from circumstances around me begins easily. It seems safe, even spiritual at first, but isolation can be a place of danger and stagnation. You order me to stay out of hiding.

I need not shrink from people. I have Your power to use in every interaction. I may feel depressed when tested, and temporarily oppressed when Satan attacks. You remind me it's okay to feel distraught at times.

You correct and guide me, not to constrain, but to train me. When situations seem overwhelming or Satan tempts me, I don't need a hiding place. I can come to You. You're my safe place always.

Psalm 32:7
You are my hiding place; You will protect me from trouble and surround me with songs of deliverance.

June 28

Trickster

Dear Jesus,

Satan's job, mighty trickster that he is, is to make me believe I'm defeated. He tries to frighten me into thinking He has authority over me and I'm powerless to resist. This bondage is illusory.

God's words to Gideon ring true for me. "The Lord is with you." Gideon named his altar, "The altar of peace." So can my life be. All turmoil ceases in Your presence.

No trickster can deceive me. I have victory through God.

Psalm 57:6,7
They spread a net for my feet— I was bowed down in distress. They dug a pit in my path— but they have fallen into it themselves. My heart, O God, is steadfast, my heart is steadfast; I will sing and make music.

June 29

Worship

Dear Jesus,

Distractions spring out of nowhere when I struggle to give my attention fully to You. Worship is sometimes a challenge. Help me, Lord. I know You dislike careless, irreverent worship.

You desire praise-filled worship. Even going through periods of dryness or sadness need not quench my spirit of worship. True worship isn't dependent on circumstances.

Jesus, guide me into focused praise. Help me avoid thoughtless words and acts. Harness my wandering mind. May my worship be a complete surrender of self-absorption. I desire to be fully present treasuring You and celebrating Your love.

Psalm 52:9
For what You have done I will always praise You in the presence of Your faithful people. And I will hope in Your name, for Your name is good.

June 30

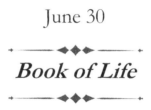

Book of Life

Dear Jesus,

How intriguing that the Book of Life contains the record of the names of all believers. Lord, You know every person who belongs to You.

The Book of Life lists the names of those in right standing who acknowledge Your saving sacrifice. Jesus, You have promised deliverance (Daniel 12:1) to everyone whose name is written there. Scripture says we will walk with You in white - You make us deserving and worthy. Our names will never be blotted out of Your book.

Jesus, I praise You that my name is in Your Book of Life. I confidently await the opening of your book and desire to be with you forever.

Revelation 3:5
The one who is victorious will, like them, be dressed in white. I will never blot out the name of that person from the book of life, but will acknowledge that name before my Father and His angels.

July 1

Longings

Dear Jesus,

Reveal Your plans for me, Jesus. Give me Your wisdom. Draw me closer.

Wants, needs and desire – Yours and mine frolic together. They're difficult to sort out sometimes, until I look deep within myself, strip away selfish motives and stifle my human pride.

Jesus, for each need met, each desire granted and each time you give me Your grace to deal with difficulty, I thank You. I long to fully honor You in all my thoughts and actions.

Psalm 20:4-5
May He give you the desire of your heart and make all your plans succeed. May we shout for joy over Your victory and lift up our banners in the name of our God. May the Lord grant all your requests.

July 2

Forever Grateful

Dear Jesus,

I don't believe I've ever thanked You…
For every gorgeous flower petal in the world,
For every bird feather enabling flight,
For every shiny fish scale in the ocean,
For each flower, bird and fish adorned in gorgeous colors,
I'm forever grateful.

Jesus, I don't believe I've ever thanked You…
For every blade of grass upon earth that pads our steps,
For every grain-bearing seed's nourishment,
For every particle of air with its precious chemical blend perfectly balanced for life.
For all these things that mean the difference between life and death, between beauty and drabness, I'm deeply grateful.

Colossians 3:16
Let the message of Christ dwell among you richly as you teach and admonish one another with all wisdom through psalms, hymns, and songs from the Spirit, singing to God with gratitude in your hearts.

July 3

Connection

Dear Jesus,

Human rejection hurts. David, as King-to-be, knew well how it felt to be hated and hunted by Saul. Job felt pain from his friends with their useless advice and condemnation. Jesus, You experienced the cruelest rejection of all. Those You walked among betrayed You without cause. Even Your closest friends deserted You.

Jesus, You understand my concern to feel accepted. I needn't worry because You promise to never reject me even if people around me do. You assure me of continual acceptance and intimate relationship forever. This means more to me than words can express.

Because of You, I have confidence and continual connection with God the Father and the Holy Spirit.

Psalm 41:12
Because of my integrity You uphold me and set me in Your presence forever.

July 4

Deception

Dear Jesus,

People who are ignorant of Your ways assume You're not loving, powerful, compassionate, trustworthy, gracious, and tender. Wonderful qualities - Jesus - You have them all!

Even Satan knows You're righteous and loving yet he tries to deceive others. He wants people frightened of You, filled with doubt and discouragement, and tricked with deceit.

I scorn Satan's deception. Jesus, You're my comfort, my strength, my healer, my hope, and my joy.

Jeremiah 33:6
Nevertheless, I will bring health and healing to it; I will heal my people and will let them enjoy abundant peace and security.

July 5

Absorbing

Dear Jesus,

I marvel at the different ways people study and apply Your Word.

Some select one special Biblical verse that's personally encouraging and call it their life verse. Others say they're standing on Your promises or hanging on Your Word.

I like absorbing as much of Your Word as possible. I read a few chapters of Scripture a day and memorize verses. I want the words to permeate every brain cell, filter every thought, and impact every action. Jesus, I treasure all these ways of applying Scripture to my life.

2 Timothy 3:16
All Scripture is God-breathed and is useful for teaching, rebuking, correcting and training in righteousness.

July 6

Wayward Will

Dear Jesus,

When I truly seek truth in Your Word it speaks to me and challenges me. I listen with my heart and learn. Your commands are clear, although difficult to apply at times.

Help me want what You want foremost and forever. You are divinely lovable and trustworthy Jesus. Your desire for my good exceeds my own.

Help me stomp out my wayward willfulness and end my occasional foolishness. I submit my will totally to Yours, precious Jesus.

Psalm 51:17
My sacrifice, O God, is a broken spirit; a broken and contrite heart You, God, will not despise.

July 7

Path of Love

Dear Jesus,

You made a new way for me, the path of love. Before You entered earth's time, forgiving an enemy was not a common thing. Nor was living without guilt. No one spoke of receiving the power of grace to forgive or the ability to live unburdened by shame and sin.

On Your path of love I see value in every person because I walk among Your beloved - You help me care because You do. I follow Holy Spirit nudges to bless and brighten others by heart touching them with acts of kindness and holy, intangible gifts - quick smiles and easy laughter. I can seek to defuse evil with good.

I trust in Your love and protection as I journey along my life's path. Help me leave behind a trail of blessings.

Romans 15:2
Let each one of us make it a practice to please his neighbor for his good and for his true welfare, to edify him [to strengthen him and build him up spiritually.]

July 8

Whatever

Dear Jesus,

I want to be a whatever and wherever person for You. Whatever You give me to do and wherever You choose to send me is fine. Beginnings and endings, joy and sorrow, living and dying - in all these I commit the circumstances and timing to You. I want to be a whatever person for You.

I'm willing, just name it, whatever I can do to fulfill Your will. As long as I'm acting through You and for You. With You as my rock and fortress whatever the future holds, I know I'll be okay.

I long to live my life Your way. Guide me firmly.

Psalm 63:1-8

I will praise you as long as I live, and in Your name I will lift up my hands. I will be fully satisfied as with the richest of foods; with singing lips my mouth will praise You. On my bed I remember You; I think of You through the watches of the night. Because You are my help, I sing in the shadow of Your wings. I cling to You; Your right hand upholds me.

July 9

Friends

Dear Jesus,

Thank you for gifting me with friends to walk with along my path of life. These friends listen to my fears, see my shortcomings and stretch their loving arms around me.

They give me priceless gifts of wisdom and encouragement. They also seek You with all their hearts. Together we work toward a life of more of You and less of us.

Because of these precious friends I move through life braver and stronger than I'd be alone. Jesus, You were so right about the value of going forth two by two.

Mark 6:7
Calling the Twelve to Him, He began to send them out two by two and gave them authority over impure spirits.

July 10

Sharing

Dear Jesus,

   Your servant Paul knew the importance of passing on the truth he knew about You to his disciple, Timothy. I also get to hand over the knowledge I've acquired. First of all, I've taught our children about You - the next generation of our family is prepared.

   I also make an effort to share You with individuals I encounter. It's exciting to find those who will embrace knowing who You are. They're blessed as I explain the gifts You give to help every person live with spiritual significance and deep purpose.

   Like Paul, I'm on the lookout for men and women who will guard this treasure of truth and share it with wisdom. Where are the Timothys who need to hear? Show me Lord.

1 Timothy 6:11-12
But you, man of God, flee from all this, and pursue righteousness, godliness, faith, love, endurance and gentleness. Fight the good fight of the faith. Take hold of the eternal life to which you were called when you made your good confession in the presence of many witnesses.

July 11

Go-To-God

Dear Jesus,

Whatever the situation I'm in, You're my Go-To-God. During pain and illness You're there. I ask for healing and/or grace to endure. You never fail me.

At times of joy and laughter You share my every delight. Falling leaves and winter snow, spring winds and summer softness. In each season I see your beauty and experience Your creation.

The ups and downs of daily life come, but I never despair. All things ultimately work for good. I treasure this truth and live with trust and confidence because of it. I can't imagine how people manage without Your help, my Go-To-God.

Psalm 22:22
I will declare Your name to my people in the assembly I will praise You.

July 12

I Hurt

Dear Jesus,

I hurt today. I feel soul-piercing pain, mental torture and oppressive anxiety. How can people I love disappoint me so? I'd hoped for different behavior. How can I risk trusting again?

Where is the power I need to forgive?

Unless You rescue me I cannot go on. Fear and anger become almost physical torture. Living is exhausting. Sleep eludes me. Help me forgive, Jesus. I know You will for I must.

Matthew 6:14
For if you forgive other people when they sin against you, your heavenly Father will also forgive you.

July 13

Balance

Dear Jesus,

I start each new day rededicating myself to You and acknowledging the day's sacredness as I venture forth serving You and encouraging others.

You bring the blessing of balance between the polarities in life, old and new, past and future. The sweetness of all our past days together is my daily joy.

You're God of all the "newness" in my life and God of all the precious "oldness" that I fondly remember. Continuity, familiarity and security flow from my relationship with You. New daily delights of excitement, adventure and surprises await me too.

Proverbs 1:5
Let the wise listen and add to their learning, and let the discerning get guidance.

July 14

Light and Laughter

Dear Jesus,

You are love. Without You, there'd be no source of love. You are light. Without You there'd be no light on earth. Your laughter was the first laughter. Without You there'd be no laughter.

Because of You my life is filled with love, light and laughter. Through You, amazing Jesus, I experience delight in my heart.

I give so little in return. Gentle God, Holy Helper, Sustaining Sprit, Transforming Trinity, all this and more You are to me. All this love, light and laughter You provide!

John 8:12
When Jesus spoke again to the people, He said, "I am the light of the world. Whoever follows me will never walk in darkness, but will have the light of life."

July 15

Anguish

Dear Jesus,

Sleep eludes me. Anguish pursues me. Maker of sunshine. Speak to me today. Darkness surrounds me, steals my voice. The energy-robber stalks me.

I pause, focus on You and remember You're here. You brighten my inner being and calm me. I sense You urge me to take control of these nasty thoughts of distress. I offer praise to You, despite the turmoil I see. Immerse me in the light of Your truth. For You Lord are the Good-maker. You ultimately make all things in my world well and right.

I need only choose to trust and rejoice. Peace returns. Praise You.

Exodus 14:31
And when the Israelites saw the mighty hand of the Lord displayed against the Egyptians, the people feared the Lord and put their trust in Him and in Moses His servant.

July 16

Grazing

Dear Jesus,

I love our middle of the night sessions, when You nudge and cajole me. I open Your Word. You bless me with Your wise thoughts.

You turn my brain loose to graze within Scripture until I find the nourishment I need. What delicious food You provide as I feast on Your truth.

Sometimes I didn't even know how hungry I was until You urged me to eat. Tasty morsels of Your wisdom feed my starving soul.

Matthew 22:29
Jesus replied, "You are in error because you do not know the Scriptures or the power of God.

July 17

Sin-taker

Dear Jesus,

Holy and beloved You call me. I'm made sin-free by You, Holiness itself.

You're my Master Tuner. I need You to tune me up often. I'm pounded upon by the drama of life and can easily succumb to sin. Without frequent re-tuning I'd be useless. Your forgiving touch upon me is kind and Your exquisite love makes fine adjustments I need. My inner self must be rechecked often.

Infuse me, permeate and energize me that I may be a living, constant symbol of Your love and sin-taking power. You fill me with joy and confidence. I square my shoulders and lift my head hearing the divine melody You've designed for Me.

Hebrews 1:3
The Son is the radiance of God's glory and the exact representation of His being, sustaining all things by His powerful word. After He had provided purification for sins, He sat down at the right hand of the Majesty in heaven.

July 18

Dual-dweller

Dear Jesus,

I've learned that life is to be lived with one foot on earth and one in the heavenlies - one eye upon Christ at all times. I'm not simply an earth-dweller.

My spirit needs continual contact with Your Holy Spirit through prayer. My prayer immediately enters the heavenlies.

I must be aware of my reality. At all times I'm a dual-dweller. Living upon earth's soil, while breathing in heaven's purified air.

Revelation 5:8
And when he had taken it, the four living creatures and the twenty-four elders fell down before the Lamb. Each one had a harp and they were holding golden bowls full of incense, which are the prayers of God's people.

July 19

Awake

Dear Jesus,

I awaken during the night with a conscious awareness of You. I wonder why I'm awake at midnight, three a.m., and five o'clock. To give You praise? To present my thoughts to You through prayer? I've no big prayer concern. No desperate need. No huge fear. No stricken loved ones. My subconscious slips into glorifying Your presence. Just enjoying time with You.

A nocturnal experience of deep joy with You while on earth. A heart-lift in your lab of love during the night. Being silent in darkness brightened by You, Lord - how awesome is this!

Psalm 5:11-12
But let all who take refuge in You be glad; let them ever sing for joy. Spread Your protection over them, that those who love Your name may rejoice in You.

What I Love

Dear Jesus,

I love living with Your Spirit who lights up my life.
I love living with holy love that makes each human
encounter an adventure.
I love that You take what's human in me and make it
divine.
I love knowing You have authority over every event.
I love that my role is simply to show up and respond
according to Your will.
I love knowing I'm eternal while still on earth.

I love you more than words can say.

Colossians 2:2
My goal is that they may be encouraged in heart and united in love, so that
they may have the full riches of complete understanding, in order that they
may know the mystery of God, namely, Christ.

July 21

Nudges

Dear Jesus,

Music-Maker, Blessing-Giver. You're my guide for yesterday, today and forever. I respond to Your Holy Spirit nudges. Lead me today through my day. I await Your moment-by-moment direction.

Graced with Your power, may each tomorrow exceed every yesterday, all purpose-driven by You. Because of Your presence with me, Jesus, I can shout with joy when others fear. I'm able to raise my head when others are bent over.

When You lead through my work and play I see fruit. This is my confidence, the mystery of submission that makes me whole and free.

Joshua 24:14-18
But as for me and my household, we will serve the Lord. Then the people answered, Far be it from us to forsake the Lord to serve other gods! It was the Lord our God Himself who brought us and our parents up out of Egypt, from that land of slavery, and performed those great signs before our eyes. He protected us on our entire journey and among all the nations through which we traveled.

July 22

More Compassion

Dear Jesus,

More compassion and less criticism! Isn't that what you want from me, from all of us? I can easily recognize another's fault, and speak a correction in my mind thinking how this person could do better. Who am I to criticize? I've certainly experienced my own frustrations when I've acted foolishly without Your guidance.

Jesus, forgive me. I often reek of pride and arrogance. I know people around me are trying their best to live good and decent lives. Every person needs encouragement far more than correction.

May I be a supporter and a nurturer, as You are.

Psalm 86:15
But You, Lord, are a compassionate and gracious God, slow to anger, abounding in love and faithfulness.

July 23

Wondering

Dear Jesus,

Anyone seeking to know if You're real needs only to walk outdoors. You're so visible in the beauty and precision of nature! Anyone confused about creation or evolution needs only look at the human body. The intricate design of every organ gives a clear answer.

Anyone wondering how to best live needs only check out Your Word. Your way of living is so wise. Love and serve others as You command or hate others like Satan? Which one feels better? Which way produces better results?

Jesus, Your reality and principles for living are unsurpassed. Your anointing is transformational making even ugly pain purposeful, and darkness brilliant. You perform wonders making enemies benefactors, gentle people powerful and the warrior a servant.

Exodus 34:10
Then the Lord said: I am making a covenant with you. Before all your people I will do wonders never before done in any nation in all the world. The people you live among will see how awesome is the work that I, the Lord, will do for you.

July 24

Imitating

Dear Jesus,

The most thrilling times of my day are when I act most like You. Serving You means following in Your footsteps and imitating Your ways in the world.

Sometimes I get to be an encourager to someone who needs affirmation. Often You urge me to offer mercy and kindness to a person who offended me. Loving like You do is my greatest delight. Oh the joy this gives me.

May I flow through my days using the gifts You've given me to bless Your people. How amazing - when I act like You I feel most like me – the me You created me to be.

1 Peter 1:12
It was revealed to them that they were not serving themselves but you, when they spoke of the things that have now been told you by those who have preached the gospel to you by the Holy Spirit sent from heaven. Even angels long to look into these things.

July 25

Waste Nothing

Dear Jesus,

Your listeners forgot all sense of time in the presence of Your divinity. They lost all thought of human nourishment as You fed their souls the richest of spiritual morsels. Then, You prepared a physical meal in a miracle manner, no less, to strengthen their bodies as well as souls.

You waited until guests ate their fill, then ordered leftovers to be collected from Your sumptuous, spontaneous feast for later use wasting nothing, not a fragment.

Obviously You don't like waste. How often do I allow my time and energy to be wasted— a collection of undone "I wills" and inadequate "I dids" and inappropriate "I saids?" Yet You draw me close, and whisper You will redeem even these times and waste nothing. Amazing!

John 6:12-15

Jesus then took the loaves, gave thanks, and distributed to those who were seated as much as they wanted. He did the same with the fish. When they had all had enough to eat, He said to His disciples, "Gather the pieces that are left over. Let nothing be wasted."

July 26

Transformation

Dear Jesus,

I read the Scripture with awe about Nicodemus who first came to see You at night, sneaking over. You intrigued him, surprised him with Your truth and changed him. Nicodemus experienced Your power as a Lifechanger. He knew human transformation is possible and amazing.

Nicodemus lived for You following his clandestine encounters with You. Emboldened, he acted on what he believed and spared no expense. After Your crucifixion in broad daylight Nicodemus fearlessly brought seventy-five pounds of myrrh and aloes to properly prepare Your body for burial. He didn't care who saw or objected.

Jesus, may Nicodemus' certitude and boldness be mine.

John 19:39-42
He was accompanied by Nicodemus, the man who earlier had visited Jesus at night. Nicodemus brought a mixture of myrrh and aloes, about seventy-five pounds. Taking Jesus' body, the two of them wrapped it, with the spices, in strips of linen. This was in accordance with Jewish burial customs. At the place where Jesus was crucified, there was a garden, and in the garden a new tomb, in which no one had ever been laid.

July 27

Our Day

Dear Jesus,

How awesome to spend my first morning moments alone with You as You guide me into plans for our day. You are my source of stability in this world of continual change. When life is unsettling, I take comfort in knowing I charge forward, buoyed by knowledge of Your constant direction and provision.

Whatever difficulty comes can be endured with Your strength. And every good experience is more delightful savored in Your presence. I'm privileged to live with this inner experience of tranquility.

You who calmed the sea, focus and direct me. I totally trust Your plans for me knowing they're always best. At evening time I say grateful prayers of praise. I peacefully enter into my rest and await a new day.

Psalm 5:3
In the morning, Lord, you hear my voice; in the morning I lay my requests before you and wait expectantly.

July 28

Bouncing

Dear Jesus,

When I awake images and ideas start to bounce in my head. A variety of imaginative thoughts frolic in my mind, from apples to bubbles, jump ropes to world peace.

Best of all are my images of You, which I savor. A cloud by day, and a fire by night. How fortunate the Israelites were to have such a visible sign of Your presence Lord!

Jesus, I follow all these tantalizing threads of thought. I enjoy the thrill of imagining. Every individual has this power of imagination, what a great gift it is. You encourage me to use mine well.

Acts 17:20
You are bringing some strange ideas to our ears, and we would like to know what they mean.

July 29

Spiritual Art

Dear Jesus,

You change hearts with infinite patience and precious tenderness. At times boldly and brusquely you transform a soul. Short and sweet or lingering and slow, always lovingly, You draw to Yourself those with ears willing to hear.

I visualize Your truth and love swirling about in human hearts as You create a spiritual work of art in each.

I see Your artistry all around me in lives You've recreated. Most of all, I love the way You work in my heart to beautify my life.

Hebrews 13:20
Now may the God of peace, who through the blood of the eternal covenant brought back from the dead our Lord Jesus, that great Shepherd of the sheep, equip you with everything good for doing His will, and may He work in us what is pleasing to Him, through Jesus Christ, to whom be glory for ever and ever. Amen.

July 30

Sparks

Dear Jesus,

You've placed a spark in each person. It comes from connection to You, the power source. In some individuals it still needs to be ignited. When the connection is strong, human spirits flare, bold and brilliant.

Once lit, the pull of selfishness dwindles. The joy of self-denial is real. You affect lives powerfully.

How beautiful are the people You indwell. Loving You brings sweetness beyond compare. Knowing You is an incredible experience of deep and constant joy.

Psalm 35:28
My tongue will proclaim Your righteousness, Your praises all day long.

July 31

Running

Dear Jesus,

Running mindlessly here and there can become habitual, fruitless as it is. Where have I been, what have I done? Jesus, do You watch and say there she goes again thinking she's accomplishing something when really it's nothing?

My life is like a criss-crossed path. I move along sometimes alone, but often touching shoulders with others in passing without noticing them. The paths split and I join new travelers. Back and forth, up and down, and round about.

Jesus, I hear You say, "Rest my child, rest in Me. Relaxation is important. Look within yourself. Find satisfaction that a busy outer life can't provide. I'm the Divine Doer. I'll guide You to do what needs doing and to times of refreshment as well."

Psalm 119:5-8
Oh, that my ways were steadfast in obeying Your decrees! Then I would not be put to shame when I consider all Your commands. I will praise You with an upright heart as I learn your righteous laws. I will obey Your decrees; do not utterly forsake me.

August 1

Who I Am

Dear Jesus,

Why am I who I am, and why are others who they are? Why do I live now in history? What purpose shall I serve? How did you decide to give me olive skin, and brown eyes, not blue? My speech is on the quiet side, my smile strong, and my brain always busy, why?

Was picking my parents tough? One knew You, one didn't. Then both. How did this happen? You chose America for my birthplace. Why Uruguay and India and Australia for other beloved children? How did you decide? My questions swirl, seeking answers.

Regardless, I'm glad that being the me I am was part of Your plan, Jesus. Because You are Who You said You were, I can be assured that I am Who You say I am. A child of the one true God born to know, love, and serve You forever. Hallelujah!

Revelation 19:6
Then I heard what sounded like a great multitude, like the roar of rushing waters and like loud peals of thunder, shouting: "Hallelujah! For our Lord God Almighty reigns."

August 2

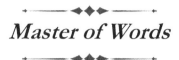

Master of Words

Dear Jesus,

Words matter. You're the Master of Words. You entered earth time as the Living Word of God.

Your Word holds meaning and power. May mine also!

I must choose my words with precision and speak with authority. I realize words are valuable only if they're matched by the integrity of my heart. Please guide me in the words I speak and write. May each word glorify You.

1 Thessalonians 2:13
And we also thank God continually because, when you received the Word of God, which you heard from us, you accepted it not as a human word, but as it actually is, the Word of God, which is indeed at work in you who believe.

August 3

Speaking Up

Dear Jesus,

You want me to deliver Your truth with decisiveness, but I'm often reluctant. You say use the qualities and gifts You've given me and speak up, but the fact is, it's often easier to remain silent.

Telling others about the love affair You have with them may seem intrusive. It makes me vulnerable, even if my only intention is to bless.

Vulnerability? Isn't that what You modeled for me every day You walked the earth? You revealed that You were God and exposed Yourself to being scoffed at and mocked. I'm in the best of company - Yours - when I allow myself to be ridiculed or ignored. Okay, I'm willing to risk being vulnerable if it saves even one soul from going to hell.

Matthew 28:19-20
Therefore go and make disciples of all nations, baptizing them in the name of the Father and of the Son and of the Holy Spirit, and teaching them to obey everything I have commanded you. And surely I am with you always, to the very end of the age."

August 4

Treasure

Dear Jesus,

You're the CEO of heaven and earth, my Lord and God and my greatest Lover. I treasure Your authority and delight in Your love.

What a privilege to be formed in Your image. You teach me clearly how to behave. I've learned greed consumes, envy destroys, and pride corrupts. Qualities like generosity enriches myself and others. Kindness blesses people and humility enhances me.

May I be mindful of these distinctions always. Your perfect example is my model.

Matthew 16:19-20
Do not store up for yourselves treasures on earth, where moths and vermin destroy, and where thieves break in and steal. But store up for yourselves treasures in heaven, where moths and vermin do not destroy, and where thieves do not break in and steal.

August 5

Agony

Dear Jesus,

I know You're present in the peace as well as the clamor of life. At this moment I taste agony. It fills and chokes me stealing my calm and stifling my peace. I'm hurt almost beyond endurance. You know my turmoil. Lift it, I pray, off my soul.

Betrayed by a friend, abused for my innocence, I tremble and hyperventilate. With the Psalmist David I cry out wrong, wrong, wronged. My trust has been misplaced, I was blinded by naiveté. I'm dreading outcomes, expecting the unacceptable and consumed by this horror of deceit.

Jesus, keep me from these energy wasters that rob me of living with the vibrancy You intend. Heal my wounds, and renew my inner confidence. Restore and brighten my countenance as only You can.

Jeremiah 4:19
Oh, my anguish, my anguish! I writhe in pain. Oh, the agony of my heart! My heart pounds within me, I cannot keep silent. For I have heard the sound of the trumpet; I have heard the battle cry.

August 6

Last Days

Dear Jesus,

The signs of the last days, which were prophesied long ago, begin to appear. Your Word of Truth is squelched. The commandments You ordained for humankind to live by are scoffed at. The beauty of sex has been desecrated by lust, the sanctity of marriage sullied. The airwaves carry despicable sounds. Truth is twisted into lies as false knowledge is presented as truth.

Pleasure that reeks of evil is embraced. Sin that destroys lives is portrayed as delectable. People cry out, "Where are You God? Make this evil stop."

You say, "Fear not. The world unfolds with evil, but You will reign one day on heaven and earth. Despair not! Trust Me." Jesus, I will!

Daniel 12:1
At that time Michael, the great prince who protects your people, will arise. There will be a time of distress such as has not happened from the beginning of nations until then. But at that time your people—everyone whose name is found written in the book—will be delivered.

August 7

Alleluia Day

Dear Jesus,

Every day is worthy of an alleluia. I have only to look closely. Always I find reasons for praise.

Yes, bad events occur, but good do as well. Streaks of courage are often birthed during fear. Sacred moments can be experienced during death watches. Tender touches are extended and treasured during tragedy. Beautiful clarity comes. Confusion turns into illumination. Every day always contains elements worthy of an alleluia.

May my heart be a holy hill, a Zion. Jesus, reside in the sanctuary of my soul as I sing alleluia for this day.

Revelation 19:1
After this I heard what sounded like the roar of a great multitude in heaven shouting: "Hallelujah! Salvation and glory and power belong to our God.

August 8

Mind of Christ

Dear Jesus,

Yours is the mind that made all minds. It's difficult for me to conceive that Your mind comprehends infinity, composed the chords forming all music and continually sustains the world.

Your mind is also the center of all wisdom and love. You loved to the point of Your death on the cross and extend forgiveness even to the yet-to-be-born.

How amazing that I have Your fantastic mind available to guide me! Incredible things happen when I interact with Your mind through reading Your Word! I'm inspired and transformed.

1 Corinthians 2:16
For, "Who has known the mind of the Lord so as to instruct him?" But we have the mind of Christ.

Ten Thousand

Dear Jesus,

You're my Make-It-Right God. For the ten thousand ways I didn't love well, You can make it right. For the ten thousand times I didn't say the right thing, You can make it right. For the ten thousand times I failed to notice a need, the many thousand times I "didn't" when I "should have," You can make it right.

Thank you for the ten thousand things I could regret if You didn't make them right! And for all those positive things You urge me to do when I act in obedience, I'm beyond grateful.

Jesus, my Make-It-Right God, ten thousand thanks!

Psalm 130:4
But with You there is forgiveness, so that we can, with reverence, serve You.

August 10

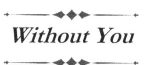

Without You

Dear Jesus,

Without You I believe the sun would seem black, bright would be dark, fun would seem senseless and laughter would sound shrill.

Without You, fear can arrive unbidden, slipping over my soul, suffocating my peace.

Without You Jesus, heaven couldn't be gained and horror upon horror, death would destroy my soul. I'm so thankful there is You!

Job 23:12
I have not departed from the commands of His lips; I have treasured the words of His mouth more than my daily bread.

August 11

Free of Self

Dear Jesus,

A pat-seeker was I. How foolish. I liked pats on my back and verbal affirmations—human acclaim attesting to my worth. Now I know Your approval alone is sufficient.

Why briefly bask in human praise when You've placed righteousness in my heart? Jesus, help me stay free of myself. The love and affirmations in Your Word are more than I need in my lifetime.

How well You know that alone I am inadequate, incomplete, and insignificant. It's You Who take away my "ins" and by Your divine mercy You make me adequate, complete and significant. I praise You Jesus for freeing me from all that I lack and becoming my sufficiency!

Galatians 5:1
It is for freedom that Christ has set us free. Stand firm, then, and do not let yourselves be burdened again by a yoke of slavery.

August 12

Holy Light

Dear Jesus,

By a single command, "Let there be light," You created brightness on earth. Your light cycled through time differentiating days and breaking the strength of darkness. Then years later, one special night, earth's light became extraordinary when the light of You in the flesh entered the world.

This light cycled through generations disturbing both kings and shepherds. It impacted humble human beings and ultimately all mankind. This holy light has never been extinguished and continuously energizes the universe, visibly and invisibly.

Jesus, I've seen Your extraordinary holy light. I've walked in its warmth and experienced its comfort. You are indeed my Soul-Brightener, the Light of the World.

John 8:12
When Jesus spoke again to the people, He said, "I am the light of the world. Whoever follows Me will never walk in darkness, but will have the light of life."

August 13

Prophecies

Dear Jesus,

The world is unfolding exactly as prophesied. Ultimately every God-inspired prophetic word will be fulfilled. A human explosion of knowledge is occurring without a foundation of wisdom. Abundant words of love are spoken without substance. Self-filled chatterings are rampant, rather than selfless concern for others and helpful deeds.

The ultimate freedom of man's will allows for many choices that can lead to heaven or hell. The power to choose must be exercised with great wisdom.

Jesus, I'm grateful that You guide my choices and guard me from senseless decisions and consequent travail. Even when the decisions of others create suffering on earth You empower me to endure. One day all prophecies will be fulfilled and You'll reign in glory and power. May it be soon!

Revelation 2:10
Do not be afraid of what you are about to suffer. I tell you, the devil will put some of you in prison to test you, and you will suffer persecution for ten days. Be faithful, even to the point of death, and I will give you life as your victor's crown.

August 14

Empowered

Dear Jesus,

You lifted Your hands to bless Your disciples and while still blessing them were taken up into heaven. Your followers worshipped You and returned to Jerusalem with great joy. They saw, felt and experienced You. They knew You personally! So, too, can I.

The disciples realized they were changed and energized. You commanded them to preach in Your name forgiveness of sins to all nations. How could Your followers manage this? Only with the power of the Holy Spirit.

They waited until they were clothed with power from on high. Then they spoke, sang, shouted and feared nothing. They knew how important it was to stay intimately connected with You through prayer. So too, must I!

Luke 24:46-50
He told them, "This is what is written: The Messiah will suffer and rise from the dead on the third day, and repentance for the forgiveness of sins will be preached in His name to all nations, beginning at Jerusalem. You are witnesses of these things. I am going to send you what My Father has promised; but stay in the city until you have been clothed with power from on high."

August 15

Repenting

Dear Jesus,

I used to be a sin expert. Now I hate sin. No one understands better than You, Jesus, how ugly sin is. Each of us is responsible for choosing our sinful behaviors. It's silly to claim there's no personal guilt or blame an external cause like heredity or society for sin.

Every sinful choice makes the next one easier by further weakening the will. Eventually morality seems foolish. Sin is excessive working, eating, drinking or other drugs. It's often cloaked in denial. Most sadly sin further separates us from You. Eventually sin creates despair that there's no hope for change.

Jesus, may every sinner respond to Your invitation to get right with You and repent. Thank You for Your willingness to forgive sinners. Guard me from every sin!

Romans 3:23
For all have sinned and fall short of the glory of God.

August 16

Your Favorite

Dear Jesus,

In my heart I hear You speak these words to me: "Precious child of mine, treasure divine, enjoy your life sublime. No one can steal the blessings from any child of Mine."

I feel like Your favorite child even though I know every other person is special too. You love all individuals equally. Nothing I could ever do would make You not love me. You gave Your life for me!

My thoughts are not prideful. I'm simply humbly grateful for the privileges You give to all Your children. Hallelujah!

Romans 5:5
And hope does not put us to shame, because God's love has been poured out into our hearts through the Holy Spirit, who has been given to us.

August 17

Surviving

Dear Jesus,

When I'm disturbed, I look for signs of Your harmony and creative splendor in nature. During times of pain creation comforts me. I gaze on giant oaks against patches of azure sky frosted with clouds. Such beauty! Oh my Jesus, Your creative Presence recreates me and minimizes my distress.

Of course I long for permanent relief. Flow into me and through me and make my pain cease. Please right the wrongs in my life. I place before You my every thought and emotion for Your gentle direction. Point out where it's me who may need to change my ways.

If I must temporarily endure this disharmony, please give me more grace-filled moments of beauty that I may survive it.

Psalm 27:4
One thing I ask from the Lord, this only do I seek: that I may dwell in the house of the Lord all the days of my life, to gaze on the beauty of the Lord and to seek Him in His temple.

August 18

Unbelief

Dear Jesus,

Sometimes I foolishly trust in my opinions and solutions instead of Your promises. When I decide Your actions are too small, too slow or Your goals for me too humble or too hard, I can react like an unbeliever.

Unbelief is unadulterated sin and atrocious betrayal of You, my Divine Savior. Unbelief says I know better than You. It says I can and must solve every situation on my own and reeks with superiority and self-delusion.

Unbelief is the result of thinking You cannot or will not help me. Jesus guard me from such heresy.

Romans 12:2
Do not conform to the pattern of this world, but be transformed by the renewing of your mind. Then you will be able to test and approve what God's will is—His good, pleasing and perfect will.

August 19

Focus

Dear Jesus,

Here I go again. Acting as if life is all about me, when I know it's not. Setting achievement goals too high that only disappoint me. How easily I slip into self-focus and subsequent stress.

My days are to be focused on You and spreading Your love and truth in the world through well-chosen words and considerate deeds. Life is not about becoming my best, but showing You're the best.

Heal my self-absorption please. Help me focus on actions of divine importance. I yearn for You to become greater as I become less. May I follow along the road You set for me.

John 3:30
He must become greater; I must become less.

Treasure Truth

Dear Jesus,

Your truth is a great treasure, given freely to me. It releases my mind from the bondage of ignorance. "My people are destroyed for lack of knowledge: because you have rejected knowledge, I will also reject you." Hosea 4:6.

Evil minds speak lies with disdain and carelessly distort truth. Truth tainted with the slightest falsehood ceases to be truth. The impurity of deception destroys it immediately. Where to find pure truth? In Your Word, the source of truth.

Jesus, You want me to guard zealously the treasure of truth that I've received. May I be a truth-seeker and truth-speaker always.

Isaiah 59:14-15
So justice is driven back, and righteousness stands at a distance; truth has stumbled in the streets, honesty cannot enter. Truth is nowhere to be found, and whoever shuns evil becomes a prey. The Lord looked and was displeased that there was no justice.

August 21

Shocking Words

Dear Jesus,

You spoke unlikely words that confounded some and delighted others:
"Take up your mat and walk."
 "Lazarus, come out."
"Peter, put away your sword."
"This day you will be with me in paradise."
"Before Abraham was born, I am."
Shocking words that transformed lives - words that thrill me every time I read them.
Jesus, I treasure Your controversial words. With them You changed the world.

John 8:58
Very truly I tell you, Jesus answered, "before Abraham was born, I am!"

August 22

Thinking

Dear Jesus,

Thinking about You is my favorite thing to do. Quiet becomes stiller, joy becomes deeper and each moment becomes richer. How satisfying! Nothing compares.

How can I describe my emotion at the very thought of You? Maybe like the first second of diving underwater into a world of stillness. Or halfway down the roller coaster when the ride is pure joy after the scary part at top.

I experience pure joy when my focus stays on you. A sensation of peace and wholeness flows through me. I feel as if I'm in the world but not of it. I'd stay suspended there forever except You bid me to tell the good news about Your love and care for Your people.

Amos 4:13
He who forms the mountains, who creates the wind, and who reveals His thoughts to mankind, who turns dawn to darkness, and treads on the heights of the earth— the Lord God Almighty is His name.

August 23

Discipline

Dear Jesus,

I've noticed that I start new projects with high goals and strong dreams. It's the diligence of continual effort that can become drudgery.

Jesus, I need help in the middle of my doing when boredom and laziness attack. Give me determined perseverance please and stay close. I especially need help when I'm weary and extra energy is demanded.

Jesus, I know life can be lived in one of two ways: with passion and purpose or with indecision and frivolity. Also, there can be two different goals: pleasure or service. Help me be disciplined and make good decisions. May I maintain my passion to accomplish all that You've established for me.

Psalm 90:17
May the favor of the Lord our God rest on us; establish the work of our hands for us— yes, establish the work of our hands.

August 24

Jump For Joy

Dear Jesus,

I love the idea of leaping for joy. The Gospel writer Luke talks about a day when people will jump and leap for joy. Earth cannot contain their happy bodies, and they must leave earth, if only for a moment ascending heavenward. What fun!

Jesus, I often feel like jumping in my heart. Mentally I leap when I think of You. I like to ponder this thought.

On the other hand, I'm also to leap for joy if I'm hassled, rejected by others, persecuted, or attacked. This is difficult but the Scripture speaks of great reward in heaven waiting for those who suffer for Your name. I'm also to consider it pure joy when I go through trials!

Luke 6:23
Rejoice in that day and leap for joy! For indeed your reward is great in heaven, for in like manner their fathers did to the prophets.

August 25

Presence

Dear Jesus,

When I'm present before You on my knees the spiritual sparks begin to fly. My mind silently shouts: You are holy, sweet, worthy, and the personification of perfection. Jesus, You speak words of love in Your gentle voice to my soul. How amazing that You would love imperfect me!

Giver of daily power, You energize me during our time together. In Your presence my life becomes activated. As I pour out my concerns I sense that You listen and care. My problems fade, my concern ends and confidence springs to life.

My inner being expresses silent awe. Your love, powerful forever, exists unbound by time or place. I sense Your presence and experience contentment.

Psalm 59:16
But I will sing of Your strength, in the morning I will sing of Your love; for You are my fortress, my refuge in times of trouble.

August 26

Many Threads

Dear Jesus,

A little assurance if You please, Jesus, a reminder that I'm fulfilling Your vision for my life. Often it seems there are many threads to pull in life and many yarns to weave. Fragments, multiple things to do pull me this way and that. At times there appear to be too many to fit neatly into place.

Details dash through my brain until I'm flustered. I become unnerved as my schedule shatters. If You please, widen the way and remove some of this prickly bramble. Remind me why I've been put in this place and that I'm capable.

I pause, breathe deeply and cry out. Your saving grace glides into this moment. Praise You. Sweet serenity soothes my spirit. Connection with You my Lord of peace brings clarity from chaos and infuses me with calm.

Isaiah 54:10
"Though the mountains be shaken and the hills be removed, yet my unfailing love for you will not be shaken nor my covenant of peace be removed," says the Lord, who has compassion on you.

August 27

Sabbath Rules

Dear Jesus,

I appreciate Your ordering Sabbath rest and modeling it for me. Had you not set requirements for rest, I'd never take a Sabbath day off. I find it hard to stop working when things still need to be done all around me.

Pharisees haughtily and foolishly misinterpreted Your observance of the Sabbath and tried to trap You with rules for its observance. You pointed out their error. Yet You made wise exceptions to observing the Sabbath.

When a human being is suffering healing prayer is never withheld. The effort involved in doing good by helping others in need is always right. As for me, I'm blessed to celebrate Your Sabbath faithfully and joyfully each week.

Mark 3:2, Mark 3:4
Some of them were looking for a reason to accuse Jesus, so they watched him closely to see if he would heal him on the Sabbath.
Then Jesus asked them, "Which is lawful on the Sabbath: to do good or to do evil, to save life or to kill?" But they remained silent.

August 28

Effort

Dear Jesus,

May I leave nothing undone that You've given me to do. The urge to accomplish comes from deep inside me. I rely on the lessons You've taught me: Greatness dwells in simplicity and power exists in humility. How true!

May I fully use your generous gifts. You encourage my setting worthwhile goals. My effort and determination are essential, for laziness accomplishes little. Praying without ceasing is also needed for bearing fruit.

May my efforts exalt You Jesus. Whatever my mouth speaks and whatever You give my hands to do I offer to You. May You be pleased with my work when we meet face to face.

Romans 14:19
Let us therefore make every effort to do what leads to peace and to mutual edification.

August 29

Without You

Dear Jesus,

Where would I be without Your ability and willingness to take my twists and wrong turns in life and graciously, skillfully make them good? My foolish choices, unprayed over decisions and stupid ideas often need reworking.

I sometimes don't try hard enough. Other times I moan over misfortune that ultimately becomes blessing.

Without You what would I do? Despair would pursue me relentlessly. Instead I need only rely on Your help and trust You, my precious Jesus.

2 Peter 1:5
For this very reason, make every effort to add to your faith goodness; and to goodness, knowledge.

August 30

Letters

Dear Jesus,

How many spiritual letters have been preserved over two thousand years, rewritten and shared with the world? I think of the letters sent by Mordecai in the book of Esther, which established the feast of Purim and ensured the freedom of the Jews from certain annihilation.

The apostolic letters sent by Paul, Peter, James, John and Jude contain words of exhortation and enrichment. These inspired letters share Your teaching and ideas. How fortunate I am to have them.

May words about You continue to be written. I pray these intimate love messages to You exalt You and bless those who read them!

Esther 9:20
Mordecai recorded these events, and he sent letters to all the Jews throughout the provinces of King Xerxes, near and far. [Purim Established]

August 31

Your Will

Dear Jesus,

Your will weaves its way through my life with wondrous complexity, yet stark simplicity.

I may thwart Your will with my wayward behavior and block its fruition with my stubbornness. Nevertheless, it moves relentlessly urging me ever forward toward all that's right and good. Always, Your will is powered by Your eternal love and directed toward my very best.

I choose to submit to Your holy will with my entire being every moment. Yet, my humanness sometimes causes me to falter. Still, I refuse to be distressed. I simply continue to place my trust in You to right my path again.

Psalm 25:8–9
Good and upright is the Lord; therefore He instructs sinners in his ways. He guides the humble in what is right and teaches them His way.

September 1

Phrases

Dear Jesus,

I value inspirational Biblical phrases that encourage me like "Speak that all may hear," "Teach that all may know," and "In all things give thanks."

Wisdom is expressed simply in these uncomplicated one-liners. I also meditate often on words from the Psalms and Proverbs.

I'm motivated by these excerpts in my humble efforts to multiply Your work in the world.

Galatians 2:2
I have been crucified with Christ and I no longer live, but Christ lives in me. The life I now live in the body, I live by faith in the Son of God, who loved me and gave Himself for me.

September 2

Healing Power

Dear Jesus,

O Jesus, essence of Godness, powerful beyond human comprehension. I need Your tornado-level force, a release of volcanic activity, in short a miracle.

I'm sad in my innermost being for My friend who suffers physically. May joy rise within this dear woman's soul and health flourish again. Exalt Your glorious name by freeing her from illness. Release Your healing power with speed, I pray.

Anoint my words to her. I know that physical healing doesn't always happen and death is not punishment but completion of one's mission on earth. May I speak words of Scripture to this woman to comfort her.

Psalm 103:2-5
Praise the Lord, my soul, and forget not all His benefits—who forgives all your sins and heals all your diseases, who redeems your life from the pit and crowns you with love and compassion, who satisfies your desires with good things so that your youth is renewed like the eagle's.

September 3

Biblical Wisdom

Dear Jesus,

Your Biblical treasure of wisdom is the perfect guide for kingdom-style living every day. The truth in the Word is for everyone from long deceived deadened intellects to serious, eager searchers. Wisdom from Scripture brings rich meaning and purpose to those seeking a good life.

The Bible is not a collection of fairy tales, as some claim, but epic tales of spiritual truth which are mysteriously transformational. An impressive variety of principles for right behavior exists within exciting stories. We need this truth for a happy life.

All of Scripture from Genesis to Revelation is the amazing story of Your love for us. Your Word demonstrates clearly You are real, loving and powerful. How I treasure reading Your Word!

2 Timothy 3:16,17
All Scripture is God-breathed and is useful for teaching, rebuking, correcting and training in righteousness, so that the servant of God may be thoroughly equipped for every good work.

September 4

Affirmation

Dear Jesus,

What do you want me to do? How may I best serve You? With my mouth filled with praise, I wait in expectation. My body kneels before You awaiting Your command.

You surprise me when You respond, "It's not what you do for me that is most important. Here is how to please Me. I want you to realize in your heart that you are My precious love, my fond delight and my infinite pleasure. It is not what you accomplish for Me that makes Me love you, but who you are. Never forget that I created you and I love you."

O Jesus, my shepherd, my King, how You affirm and bless me!

2 Samuel 14:17
And now your servant says, May the word of my lord the king secure my inheritance, for my lord the king is like an angel of God in discerning good and evil. May the Lord your God be with you.

September 5

Scurry

Dear Jesus,

Activities beckon me every second. I rush, dash, twirl, scurry like a squirrel. Do, did, done is my mantra, sometimes without regard for whether an activity is rewarding or fun. Jesus, You never said life would be a race, so why do I maintain this pace? I must watch where I tread, lest I end up too soon dead.

Sweet Jesus, guard my soul. Take my heart, lest the world break it, hide it in Your Kingdom chest. I am nothing without Your presence and protection.

Keep me shining and pure, away from sin's allure. My primary concern is pleasing You.

Philippians 2:13
For it is God who works in you to will and to act in order to fulfill His good purpose.

September 6

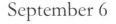

Names

Dear Jesus,

Jesus, all the earth was made through Your creativity and named by You. Dry ground You called land. Gathered waters You called seas. Simple one-syllable words. Darkness You called night and light you called day. Perfect names given by You, the perfect Name-Giver.

You allowed Adam the privilege of naming the livestock, the birds in the sky and all the wild animals. He handled his task quite well, in my opinion.

I love to meditate on the many names people call You: Lamb of God, Shepherd, King, Redeemer, Soul-Rescuer, Life-Restorer and Resurrection-Maker. Appropriate and true! Most of all, I delight in knowing You have a new name for me - Your beloved child.

Deuteronomy 18:5
For the Lord your God has chosen them and their descendants out of all your tribes to stand and minister in the Lord's name always.

September 7

Spirit Rescue

Dear Jesus,

Life hurts. Where are Your arms? My problems seem unsolvable. I need eagle's wings to soar away from them, but have none. Call your angels forth to rescue me. Verbal rocks from friends and enemies rip into my flesh. My plans shred into pieces.

Faith, fear and hope flutter together. I force myself to gasp Your name and believe my rescue will be forthcoming, even if slow in appearing. I rely on my word weapons: Alleluia! Jesus! Abba Father! Amen! Selah (So be it!) Words of faith I speak into my reality.

Holy Spirit, I cannot glorify the Father without Your help. Your power is required. Divine intervention is necessary. Empower me to survive this onslaught.

Acts 1:8
But you will receive power when the Holy Spirit comes on you; and you will be my witnesses in Jerusalem, and in all Judea and Samaria, and to the ends of the earth.

September 8

Spirit Sounds

Dear Jesus,

These are sounds of Your Spirit I love to hear:
A poor person eats.
A pastor counsels.
A friend listens.
A child receives instruction.
A son is rebuked.
A lonely woman hears comfort.
A depressed person opens a door to light.
A sick person prays for healing.
A grieving spouse laughs again.

I love their sweet melody. Thus may the Spirit speak today.

Acts 2:33
Exalted to the right hand of God, he has received from the Father the promised Holy Spirit and has poured out what you now see and hear.

September 9

Voices

Dear Jesus,

It's intriguing to think of similarities between the wind, Your voice and my testimony for You.

The wind seems to whisper in a breeze and other times to roar. Your voice speaking within me at times seems like a whisper and occasionally a roar.

Likewise, on some occasions I talk about You quietly in my normal voice and sometimes I speak loud and strong. May my voice vary appropriately when I speak of You to others. I want to speak with the variety and authority best for every situation that listeners may clearly hear.

Psalm 29:3
The voice of the Lord is over the waters; the God of glory thunders, the Lord thunders over the mighty waters.

September 10

Prayer Power

Dear Jesus,

Through prayer You enable me to have sweet encounters with You. How I love these intimate moments. In the most ordinary task, suddenly I can have contact with You. Sometimes I'll catch a glimpse of the sky and breathe out a prayer of praise. Or someone in need may come to mind and I pray. During these moments of exaltation I'm fully aware of Your divine Presence.

I pray for Your will to be accomplished in every person and every situation, and in mine as well. This helps me endure daily challenges with perseverance. I place my faith in You, believe for the unbelievable and ignore disturbing negatives. I've seen prayer unleash miracles –more potent than nuclear power.

Into Your Presence, I come and focus my prayer. From Your Presence, I'm renewed and go forward. Jesus, how amazing prayer power is!

2 Chronicles 6:19
Yet, Lord my God, give attention to your servant's prayer and his plea for mercy. Hear the cry and the prayer that your servant is praying in your presence.

September 11

Glow

Dear Jesus,

In You, through You and for You. The very thought of these words excites me and makes me feel a glow within.

I know this glow is common among Your believers and Holy Spirit-indwelled followers. The glow You bring to each life is amazing Lord. It sweetens spirits and lights the ground I walk upon.

Only You give the glow that never fades. I'm told occasionally that I'm radiant. I smile and say "It's the light of Christ within that gives me this glow." It's You Jesus.

Ezekiel 8:2
I looked, and I saw a figure like that of a man. From what appeared to be His waist down he was like fire, and from there up His appearance was as bright as glowing metal.

September 12

Essence

Dear Jesus,

You're my rock, shield and wisdom as described in Psalm 92. You're my sun of Psalm 84. You're my dwelling place of Psalm 90. You're my comfort, my righteousness and my provision. You're God beyond comprehension and all these things You are to me.

Living at Your side assures perfect peace. Jesus, great Grace-Giver, You're the essence of tenderness, sweet mountain of mercy and dispenser of exquisite justice. You are good nearly beyond belief, but believe I do.

Purpose my life according to Your pleasure and through Your grace. Empower my soul with Your zeal. Fight my foes with Your fierceness. Pierce my heart with Your truth as You guide me on my path toward eternity with You.

Psalm 91:1-2
He who dwells in the secret place of the Most High Shall abide under the shadow of the Almighty. I will say of the Lord, "He is my refuge and my fortress; My God, in Him I will trust." Surely He shall deliver you from the snare of the fowler and from the perilous pestilence.

Woodworking

Dear Jesus,

I ponder the physical work You did as You spent time on earth as a carpenter. You were comfortable handling carpenter's tools. Your hands may have been callused from laboring as a woodworker. You tread daily on sawdust and wood shavings.

Jesus, I've no doubt You performed manual effort with skill and dignity as You did everything. Yet, You were born to create not with wood and nails but with eternal love and redeeming truth. Those hands that pierced wood with nails were sadly later pierced by nails.

Woodworking Son of God! You left your carpentry to mold the apostles and all of us, crafting us for divine use.

Mark 6:3
Isn't this the carpenter? Isn't this Mary's son and the brother of James, Joseph, Judas and Simon? Aren't His sisters here with us? And they took offense at Him.

September 14

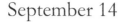

Fullness of Joy

Dear Jesus,

Scripture tells me I've been created to live in the fullness of joy in Your presence. Yet how easily I lose my steady flow of sparkle. I get involved in activities that give a superficial sense of satisfaction, but I become distracted from doing what's best. How quickly I clog my flow of joy with worldly longings by focusing on surface pleasures, while ignoring You, my deep, divine treasure.

Sadly, I often neglect to share living water with those around me who thirst for You. You give me a jolt of reality to remind me that's what my real life is to be about.

Jesus, help me continually be mindful that fullness of joy is living in Your presence and fulfilling Your will. This assures me of pleasures forevermore.

Psalm 16:11
You will show me the path of life; In Your presence is fullness of joy. At Your right hand are pleasures forevermore.

September 15

Do-er

Dear Jesus,

I'm a goal-setter, a great dreamer and a busy do-er. Yet I sometimes get too caught up in my doing and behave poorly as You well know. Pride flares when I'm criticized. Selfishness roars up if my measure is less than another's. My tendency to resentment bristles. Sins of self arise oh so quickly. I must flee their tentacles.

Only You, Jesus, know my inner ugliness that roars for attention. You see the temptations that tangle my thoughts and the self-centeredness seeking to be soothed. You've sent the Holy Spirit to battle on my behalf. Help me elicit victory from this pull toward self indulgent sin.

I long to be a holy do-er for You. Thank You for giving me both peace and purpose.

Ephesians 4:23
And be constantly renewed in the spirit of your mind – having a fresh mental and spiritual attitude.

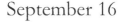

Frothy Words

Dear Jesus,

Frothy words are cheap and often careless. Their speakers express fluffy thoughts, which require no reflection. Such arguments are flimsy in content as particles of air, and just as plentiful. Frothy words assault hearers' ears with senseless chatter.

In contrast speakers of substance thrust powerful words like a lance. They pierce deceit with God's Word. Their minds have been molded through reading Scripture and letting it permeate every brain cell and filter every thought.

Jesus, may I speak solid words of power based on Scriptural truth.

Psalm 19:14
Let the words of my mouth and the meditation of my heart be acceptable in Your sight, O Lord, my Strength and my Redeemer.

September 17

Underworked Angels

Dear Jesus,

Do unprayed prayers result in underworked angels who wait on the sidelines to minister? Angels appear eager to go into immediate action after being sent by divine command. Often human requests must be made first and orders executed by You. Angel assignments are made as You see fit.

Does busy angelic activity proliferate on earth today? I like to contemplate how much goes on behind the scenes, unseen by humans.

Jesus, please send angelic help to anyone in need. Let there be ever more angelic interventions.

Psalm 103:20
Bless the Lord, you His angels, who excel in strength, who do His word, heeding the voice of His Word.

September 18

Truth Teachers

Dear Jesus,

Where are all the godly teachers? Who will step up? The spiritual vocabulary of many is meager and theological thoughts are limited and confused because not enough excellent teaching is available to Your people.

Culture promotes finding happiness in the accumulation of things instead of processing thoughts and ideas and seeking enriching relationships. Sadly many adults believe extravagant toys and possessions will give the greatest joy. They perish in their ignorance.

You desire truth-teachers who will pass on the spiritual knowledge every souls needs for eternal happiness. Jesus, may I be one. May we all.

Ephesians 4:11
And He Himself gave some to be apostles, some prophets, some evangelists, and some pastors and teachers …

September 19

Gasping

Dear Jesus,

I've overdone it again. I know this cycle. Busyness has ensnared me. I've been here before. Mentally racing, barely breathing, starving my soul until spiritual instinct triggers alarm.

I'm gasping for You Jesus, eager to breathe in the calm You alone give. I stop and wait until the breath of Your Holy Spirit revives me.

Moving at Your gentle, consistent pace is the only way to keep my peace. May I continuously be mindful of staying in harmony with You.

Matthew 11:28-30
Come to Me, all you who labor and are heavy laden, and I will give you rest. Take My yoke upon you and learn from Me, for I am gentle and lowly in heart, and you will find rest for your souls. For My yoke is easy and My burden is light.

Divine Love

Dear Jesus,

Your loving presence in the world permeates everything, even me. Amazingly, You've assured me I can be a conduit for Your divine love.

I'm love-filled to overflowing because You've given me all the love I need. Even if no other human love is ever present in my life, I'm complete forever knowing that I'm Your dearly loved child.

This is the most joyous and valuable truth I know. I want to tell everyone I meet that Your love is exquisite and available to all.

Jeremiah 31:3
The Lord has appeared of old to me, saying: "Yes, I have loved you with an everlasting love; Therefore with lovingkindness I have drawn you."

September 21

Sin So Sweet

Dear Jesus,

Sin, oh so sweet, beckons to be embraced. I've been there, tried it and want no further part. I know that sin turns like a viper stealing my inner peace and joy. Sin consumes me with obsessive pulls and stinks with polluted desires. Sin, oh so bitter, I choose to flee even the tiniest of your tentacles.

Jesus, You know the ugliness of sin – how it roars for attention, brings temptations that tangle thoughts, and nurtures self-centeredness screaming to be soothed.

You know because You battled against sin on my behalf, and helped me elicit eternal victory. Thank You Lord!

Genesis 4:7
If you had done the right thing, you would be smiling; but because you have done evil, sin is crouching at your door. It wants to rule you, but you must overcome it.

September 22

Idols

Dear Jesus,

Often people long to be like someone else or live another person's life. Why? Is this the reason people honor idols and adopt without thinking the customs of personalities in our culture? Such dissatisfaction can lead to rebellion against the values and plans of You, our Creator.

Jesus, You've made us to be unique, not to imitate another. Why abandon our specialness to be common?

It's senseless to honor earthly models rather than You. Help me guard my mind and heart from human idols. I choose You.

Ezekiel 14:6-8
Now then, tell the Israelites what I, the Sovereign Lord, am saying: "Turn back and leave your disgusting idols. Whenever one of you Israelites or one of you foreigners who live in the Israelite community turn away from me and worship idols, and then go to consult a prophet, I, the Lord, will give you your answer! I will oppose you.. that all of you will know that I am the Lord."

September 23

Rescue

Dear Jesus,

Like David, the author of the Psalms, I occasionally feel a need to express my anguish. Today, I'm cringing with chagrin, engulfed in embarrassment, and heckled by harassment. I'm drained by disappointment, frazzled by frustration, and confused by the commotion around me in this rough world, filled with real evil.

Jesus, I sense You're smiling as You tell me to stop and refocus. I don't need to fall into the pit of negativity that's open before me. Your Holy Spirit will empower me to end these unsettling thoughts and emotions.

Jesus, I've been here before and You rescued me. I don't need to continue in this morass. You're my shield, strength, and security. I won't succumb when I can overcome.

Jeremiah 1:19
"They will fight against you but will not overcome you, for I am with you and will rescue you," declares the Lord.

September 24

Brushes

Dear Jesus,

Sometimes I hold vengeful thoughts. Harboring harshness is my desire. I know vengeance is ultimately Yours, but in this moment it seems a long way off. I savor the idea of quick condemnation for those who have wronged me.

Do I truly need to allow You to brush away my anger and hurt? Yes! And I will! Swiftly Your grace banishes my wounded critical and judging spirit. You brush me with smooth, kind strokes of understanding and forgiveness.

How does this happen? Grace, incredible power that it is, removes my vindictiveness, and makes me feel loving and balanced again. You're amazing.

Mark 11:25
And when you stand praying, if you hold anything against anyone, forgive them, so that your Father in heaven may forgive you your sins."

September 25

Amaze

Dear Jesus,

Amaze me today as only You can. I walk, ponder and see all You've created for me. The sting of a bee fascinates me. The graceful movement of a deer enthralls me. The plops of raindrops delight. The warmth of the sun embraces me.

Simple, ordinary things bring me joy – peppermint, honey, tea and toast. I'm blessed by sunrises and sunsets, lemon and lavender, society and solitude, children and grandchildren, writing and reading, thinking and doing, Isaiah and Revelation, James and Jude. In every experience I glimpse Your amazing personality.

A trillion wonders to behold, a zillion stories to be told. A gazillion miracles unfold. All through You and in You.

Habakkuk 1:5
And be utterly amazed. For I am going to do something in your days that you would not believe, even if you were told.

September 26

Moment Mosaics

Dear Jesus,

Is anything more potent than a moment? A dot of time filled with possibilities. Love to be shown, actions to be performed, skirmishes to be won and ideas to be explored – all in moment.

Forever is but a collection of moments strung together as precious pearls. The essence of God's Kingdom exists on the filament of moments of now.

Jesus, You make my life a marvelous mosaic of moments, some beautiful, some broken, like my obvious shortcomings and griefs. You shape each into a vibrant whole. The new creation You make from these moments glows more richly than I could ever have imagined. You're the artist of my experiences. With You all my beautiful and broken fragments become a moment-by-moment work of divine art.

2 Corinthians 5:17
Therefore, if anyone is in Christ, the new creation has come: The old has gone, the new is here!

September 27

Sharing Love

Dear Jesus,

Mindful of Your presence, I listen to You speak. I sense Your approval when I tell others about You. I love to know I'm loved by You and love to serve You by sharing the joy of loving You with everyone I meet.

Sadly, I witness self-love in those who are consumed by self and don't know about sacrificial loving. All their motives read me and mine. The joy of service eludes them. The reality of actual love is nowhere about because self-love is false, not love at all, but pride.

Compassion is the Christian response to those consumed in self. That's Your kind of love Jesus. Not only do I love You, but I love others more deeply because of You. I long for the day all will know Your incredible love.

Ephesians 4:32
Be kind and compassionate to one another, forgiving each other, just as in Christ God forgave you.

September 28

Prayer Power

Dear Jesus,

Prayer has no parameters of time or space. Like a shaft of laser power, prayer can penetrate problems and facilitate positive outcomes. Prayer pierces bonds of evil with holiness.

Prayer can conquer pain. It holds the seeds of miracles. Prayer can transform captives of sin into new beings of holy value. Prayer fosters wisdom and makes a path for peace to come.

Prayer can smash selfish goals and make dreams arise. How does prayer makes all this possible? Supernatural power surges with action. All this happens, Jesus, because of, and through, Your power.

1 Kings 9:3
The Lord said to him: "I have heard the prayer and plea you have made before Me; I have consecrated this temple, which you have built, by putting my Name there forever. My eyes and My heart will always be there."

September 29

Cloths of Caring

Dear Jesus,

Please help those I love. Bathe them in holiness, and wrap them in invisible cloths of caring. I visualize them in garments made of fabric, soft like silk, but molded firm, like iron, letting no evil penetrate.

Thank you, Jesus, for these imaginary cloths. Those I pray for are very dear to me. I know they're even more precious to You. Nothing but divine cloths of caring will do.

I ask You, Jesus, to wrap them up. I know You hear.

Philippians 4:1
Therefore, my brothers and sisters, you whom I love and long for, my joy and crown, stand firm in the Lord in this way, dear friends!

Pure Mystery

Dear Jesus,

What total, pure, holy mystery! The power of Your crucifixion and the shedding of Your blood removes my sin and sanctifies my soul. How it works I don't know, but it amazes me. I know the process was ordained by divine intention and is made possible by supernatural intervention.

Jesus, You spoke of being living water to nourish me. I frolic in the invisible droplets that have changed my life. I revel in the gift of Your Spirit fortifying me and every believer.

You alone determine all my comings and goings and make them purpose laden. You're the giver of my every breath, and the utmost Lover of my soul. It's no mystery You're the One I want to serve forever.

Isaiah 58:11
The Lord will guide you always; He will satisfy your needs in a sun-scorched land and will strengthen your frame. You will be like a well-watered garden, like a spring whose waters never fail.

October 1

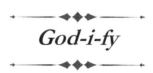

God-i-fy

Dear Jesus,

How nice it would be to have love that is limitless and the grace of super-human endurance. I'd like to exhibit kindness always, expecting nothing in return. And also gentleness that's more powerful than strength. I'd like to have the courage to ignore any earthly consequences that would interfere with being my best self. Jesus, it's obvious nothing less than a Divine fill-up will do.

I'd appreciate it if You would God-i-fy all my emotions, my thoughts, and my actions. Please God-i-fy my loving, giving and my receiving.

Permeate all of me with more of You. Nothing less than a divine fill-up will do.

1Peter 3:8
Finally, all of you, be like-minded, be sympathetic, love one another, be compassionate and humble.

October 2

Mental Lifting

Dear Jesus,

I visualize prayer in my mind's eye. I lift each person I love up to Your throne of grace. I see Your rays of mercy, strong like the sun, penetrating each of them.

Jesus, I long for You to answer my prayers for these dear ones using Your incomparable power. I'm grateful for the privilege of asking for Your tender care upon those I love.

You alone have the ability to save, to transform, to heal. You can help them meet every need. I depend on You to take care of each person I love. Praise You! Thank You.

Mark 11:24
Therefore I tell you, whatever you ask for in prayer, believe that you have received it, and it will be yours.

October 3

Great Riches

Dear Jesus,

Your Word teaches that greed consumes, envy destroys, and pride corrupts people. Yet generosity enriches, kindness blesses and humility enhances. These are clear distinctions. May I be mindful of my motives and desires during my moments of choice.

The greatest of riches can never be bought. Intimate relationship with You is priceless. Knowledge of You Jesus is invaluable. Both are free and available to all.

Because of You I can be rich in mercy, peace and love. Amazingly, this is my glorious inheritance through You. What precious treasure!

Ephesians 1:18
I pray that the eyes of your heart may be enlightened in order that you may know the hope to which he has called you, the riches of His glorious inheritance in His holy people.

October 4

Meaning-Maker

Dear Jesus,

You're the Meaning-Maker who loves and laughs, blesses and consoles, and desires to make every life a triumph. You're the Savior who walked among us and will return.

You're the Soul-Enricher who lifts human beings from the slough of selfishness and makes jewels of our acts of kindness. Creative-Maker of the wonders of the world, and all that is and all who are! You're the Love-Designer who makes monuments of love within human hearts.

For those who know You intimately, Jesus, descriptive words are unnecessary. For those repulsed at Your name, no words will be enough. Hardness of head and heart requires divine demolition. I pray that, for those who scorn Your existence, belief that You're the Meaning-Maker will spring forth.

Psalm 107:8
Let them give thanks to the Lord for His unfailing love and His wonderful deeds for mankind.

October 5

Soul Writing

Dear Jesus,

You're writing on my soul and producing a book the world can read. Daily, Lord, You decide what chapter will be written. I co-operate best by ignoring the clamor of culture around me and focusing on the purposes of Your Spirit.

For Your soul writing to succeed, I need to suppress my foolish desires. You hold mighty power to change my ways that need redirection. Jesus, I look at Your pace when You walked earth and study it. What a smooth flow to Your days, You never seemed in a hurry as I often am. Jesus, may I develop a relaxed inner spirit controlled by Your Spirit.

May only Your goals for me prevail. Master Story-Writer, write on.

2 Corinthians 5:9
So we make it our goal to please Him, whether we are at home in the body or away from it.

Joys

Dear Jesus,

I love the normal daily experiences of living. The truest joys are simple. The little things of life become big. Sunsets and sun-risings, smiles and kind gestures.

One thing is needed - my decision to find delight in You Jesus, Your people and Your world and seek it again and again. Why did I wish for the emptiness of personal gain for so long?

Like the lily, I'm completely content. Humbly, I have the privilege of serving You by sending forth Your words of truth as messengers. I pray they light fire in hearts ready to blaze. May others learn that joy in You is more than enough.

Matthew 6:28
And why do you worry about clothes? See how the flowers of the field grow. They do not labor or spin.

October 7

Spirit-plosion

Dear Jesus,

You began a huge explosion within me on the day I first knew the Holy Spirit was real. How thrilling when I truly understood Spirit-filling and experienced Spirit baptism.

All the world changes when seen via the Holy Spirit. Life bursts with purpose. Your Spirit releases enormous energy.

Life is a fantastic adventure lived with the Father, Son and Holy Spirit - Divine Comforter and Exquisite Counselor. I fall prostrate with gratitude. How privileged I am to know You, Jesus, and be empowered by Your Holy Spirit. How blessed I am to be Yours.

Matthew 3:11
I [John the Baptist] baptize you with water for repentance. But after me comes one who is more powerful than I, whose sandals I am not worthy to carry. He will baptize you with the Holy Spirit and fire.

October 8

Purpose

Dear Jesus,

All that is, has a purpose and a function. It's impossible to imagine tables without legs, yo-yos without strings, dogs without barks, books without thoughts, me without You, Jesus.

You've provided all I need to give my life purpose: structure, meaning, redemption from self-exaltation, freedom from angry retorts and mean-spirited envy, rescue from personal fears and release from despair and self-condemnation.

You're the amazing Creator and Sustainer of all the Universe, Covenant-Maker with man, and the Great Omega to every life. That it's Your purpose to dwell in my heart is an exquisite, sweet mystery to me.

Psalm 49:15
But God will redeem me from the realm of the dead; He will surely take me to Himself.

October 9

Heaven Awaits

Dear Jesus,

There's more world than what I can see, an atmosphere above and beyond all that I know. This heavenly destination abounds in love, joy and peace. It holds great allure and excites me. Thoughts of eternity comfort me during inevitable trials of life.

I love knowing heaven awaits my arrival on the day You've chosen for my entrance, Jesus. I'll enter holding Your hand. The thought of being with You, Jesus, forever is oh so sweet.

Until then I'm content serving You in the here and now. Wherever I am and You are will be Your kingdom on earth.

Isaiah 42:5
This is what God the Lord says— the Creator of the heavens, who stretches them out, who spreads out the earth with all that springs from it, who gives breath to its people, and life to those who walk on it.

October 10

Tree

Dear Jesus,

How could it be that You were placed on a tree for Your death? You created the essence of treeness. Your limbs were nailed to the cross and You became a spectacle to the world. If the tree from which the wood of the cross was made could speak would it scream at being so misused?

Jesus, You were made into a person of derision by human hate. All the while You displayed humble acceptance of Your fate. Angels stood alert, forbidden to interfere. Disciples watched in horror not comprehending. Oh the incomprehensible love of such a sacrifice.

The tree from which the wood of the cross was made became the first altar for You, my Savior.

Matthew 13:41
The Son of Man will send out His angels, and they will weed out of His kingdom everything that causes sin and all who do evil.

October 11

Acceptance

Dear Jesus,

I grumble and stumble over blocks in my plans. Physical and spiritual hurdles abound. Lift me up, Jesus. Help me clear my road and continue along, mindful as I do, never blocking another's way.

My model is Paul who never complained, nor shall I. Paul kept his life plain and simple. He shared the good news about You bravely and directly. He trusted You implicitly. He feared not and loved well.

Paul didn't beat himself up when things didn't go perfectly but accepted hardships and kept on going. Plain and simple acceptance is powerful. Help me keep my focus clear and simple and keep on moving forward.

1 Corinthians 10:10
And do not grumble, as some of them did—and were killed by the destroying angel.

October 12

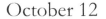

Sky-diving

Dear Jesus,

In my imagination You take me skydiving and hold me tightly while I ride on the wind. I sing of Your truth midst the stars.

Jesus, in my imagination You take me running along perilous paths through fire holding my hand. You lead me to rivers of overflowing water. I frolic in the waves.

Jesus, I can soar with a sense of purpose, flying free without fear toward my eternal destiny. Soaring with You, real or imagined, is My deepest delight!

Psalm 66:8-12
Praise our God, all peoples, let the sound of His praise be heard; he has preserved our lives and kept our feet from slipping. For you, God, tested us; you refined us like silver. You brought us into prison and laid burdens on our backs. You let people ride over our heads; we went through fire and water, but you brought us to a place of abundance.

October 13

Hovering

Dear Jesus,

You hover over me, always near. Your Presence comforts me. I'm acutely aware of Your love. When I seek Your counsel it's readily available. You treat me as Your precious creation.

Jesus, how can it be that You should love me so greatly? I'm so ordinary. But Jesus, You've also made me deep, decisive and daring. Especially in applying Your principles, and boldly speaking of You.

Jesus, I ponder that Your holy places were unlikely locations: ark on a cart, the soul of Saul, the valley known as Kidron and, wonder of wonders, within me. I delight in bowing my knee to You as You hover near me.

Isaiah 31:5
Like birds hovering overhead, the Lord Almighty will shield Jerusalem; he will shield it and deliver it, he will 'pass over' it and will rescue it.

October 14

Mighty Battle

Dear Jesus,

I wish it wasn't true, but the fact is I tend to be a sinner. I intend to do good, but easily lean toward evil, selfish, behavior, and can succumb to sinning.

Sin purging and life purifying is essential. I need to do both regularly. Confession is essential. I'm grateful that I can walk free of condemnation by Your grace.

Jesus, the spiritual battle is mighty. Satan, the evil soul-seeker wants mine. You promise me munitions of grace and Your Word of truth. The power to overcome exists. My victory is assured as I fight my battles using spiritual weapons. Jesus, thank You for always helping me.

Psalm 70:4
But may all who seek you rejoice and be glad in you; may those who long for your saving help always say, "The Lord is great!"

October 15

Tests

Dear Jesus,

Spiritual tests and trials distress me. I pray for the faith to hold strong. I understand tests have a purpose. Going through difficult experiences makes me tougher. Still I don't like this.

Trials challenge my spiritual strength. Knowing they're inevitable inspires me to stay prepared. Jonah and Job endured huge challenges. Noah had to disregard mocking people. Dealing with cruel sarcasm can be one of the hardest trials of all.

Jesus, I'd prefer not to be tested, but since You allow it for my good, I pray I'll pass with high grades. I'm encouraged to know I can depend on You to never allow me to have more challenges than I can manage.

Exodus 20:20
Moses said to the people, "Do not be afraid. God has come to test you, so that the fear of God will be with you to keep you from sinning."

October 16

Security

Dear Jesus,

I imagine Your strong arms around me making me feel safe. Sweet security! I celebrate You. Strike the silver match. Light the internal torch. My Beloved guards me!

Jesus, occasionally my feelings of security and safety seem to momentarily disappear. I can be unpredictable and flighty. Emotions rise, then quickly deflate. Life seems to be a hop from valley to mountaintop. My soul smiles, and then my heart breaks. Tears come in torrents.

But I move past my feelings and look again at Your core of truth. Soon joy emerges again. I laugh. Through it all, I'm able to trust. My soul slips into calm as I meditate on Your explicit assurance: "I will keep in perfect peace, Whoever dwells on Me." Jesus, I do. Sweet stability!

Isaiah 26:3
You will keep in perfect peace those whose minds are steadfast, because they trust in you.

October 17

Prayer Music

Dear Jesus,

You make music in my heart. I join in the song of the universe – the music initiated by You, source of all melody, heard and unheard. Sweet chords of exquisite heavenly harmony bathe me. The longer I think on You, the more the sound intensifies.

Jesus, You gift me with our musical moments of intimacy. I'd like to remain in this state forever but You recharge me with Your energy and call me into action.

I'm refreshed and strengthened and ready again for active ministry. What a joy to bring Your music everywhere I go during this concert of life. You conduct my symphony of living as You prepare my soul for the music of heaven.

2 Chronicles 5:13
The trumpeters and musicians joined in unison to give praise and thanks to the Lord. Accompanied by trumpets, cymbals and other instruments, the singers raised their voices in praise to the Lord and sang: "He is good; His love endures forever." Then the temple of the Lord was filled with the cloud.

October 18

Options

Dear Jesus,

So many career options! One friend is a welder and another a fitness coach. I'm a writer. We all have roles humbly helping Your people. No position is loftier than another.

As a writer I search my brain for ideas and form concepts using alphabet letters to nail down thoughts. I work passionately to communicate with clarity whatever You've given me to share for the benefit of others.

Holy Spirit, I hold my pen and click my keyboard, but You make ideas come and words flow. Without You nothing of value is produced. May I anoint my readers with grace, fire them with your truth.

Habakkuk 2:2
Write down the revelation and make it plain on tablets so that a herald may run with it.

Truth

Dear Jesus,

Who speaks to the Lord? I do. Who listens to the Lord? I do. Who loves the Lord and His truth? I do.

Who has faith in the Lord? I do. Faith is belief in what is unseen and not fully understood. Living my natural life requires faith. Who can explain the flight of an airplane, yet boldly I step aboard and fly. Who can make the sun rise or set? Yet I depend upon its warmth and beauty. Jesus, I believe in You because I've experienced Your reality.

I worship You! I want to live my life exalting You and Your truth - I treasure Your Word and delight in Your teaching. I take pleasure in speaking Your truth. My entire being embraces it and endeavors to guard it. Your truth is the solid rock beneath the structure of faith.

John 8:32
Then you will know the truth, and the truth will set you free.

October 20

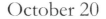

Stability

Dear Jesus,

You're my source of stability in this world of continual change. When life is unsettling, I remember that You're unchangeable. You who calmed the sea can surely calm me. Gracious giver of internal rest, You desire only the best for me. I charge into every day secure in Your unfolding plan for me.

Many consider Your commands cumbersome and outdated. Not I Lord. Psalm 19 calls Your commands radiant. They give light to the eyes and are considered more precious than gold, and sweeter than honey. How I agree! Your commands are pure gifts.

Jesus, You never leave me or disappoint me on my life journey. You say "Obey. Be safe, be well, You're mine."

Psalm 19: 8-11
The commands of the Lord are radiant, giving light to the eyes. The fear of the Lord is pure, enduring forever. The decrees of the Lord are firm, and all of them are righteous. They are more precious than gold, than much pure gold; they are sweeter than honey, than honey from the honeycomb. By them your servant is warned; in keeping them there is great reward.

October 21

Holy Urges

Dear Jesus,

I understand myself better through knowledge of Your Word. I study with the aid of Your Holy Spirit. Sometimes my progress seems slow, and more effort is needed, but I move forward.

Diligence is essential. Spiritual study of Your Word requires commitment. Without determination I might slip into lethargy and find excuses to avoid my reading. I know that to ignore Your Word is to forsake the advance of my soul.

Your Holy Spirit, pure and holy, urges me on. With the depths of Your wisdom, You see the depths of me. I'm grateful for Your Spirit's anointing and humbled by Your indwelling Holy Spirit. Please continue to stir my soul forever through Your Word.

1 Corinthians 2:7-11
No, we declare God's wisdom, a mystery that has been hidden and that God destined for our glory before time began. None of the rulers of this age understood it, for if they had, they would not have crucified the Lord of glory. However, as it is written: "What no eye has seen, what no ear has heard, and what no human mind has conceived" -the things God has prepared for those who love him— these are the things God has revealed to us by His Spirit.

October 22

Message Bearers

Dear Jesus,

Ezekiel, Jeremiah and Isaiah had ears tuned to Divine communication and they spoke words with authority regardless of the consequences. These Old Testament prophets and mighty servants of truth spoke of freedom's promise for a time yet to come.

Sadly these message bearers were often persecuted for their faithfulness. Nevertheless they felt compelled to continue to serve. Each learned that service often required sacrifice and obedience could bring unpopularity. Their work demanded commitment and they gave it. Prophetic truth marched forward unstoppable. These prophets impacted the world in their day. They impact it still.

Jesus, Your plan continues to unfold. May I, too, speak Your truth even when it's uncomfortable or makes me unpopular.

Acts 7:52
Was there ever a prophet your ancestors did not persecute? They even killed those who predicted the coming of the Righteous One. And now you have betrayed and murdered him—

October 23

Compliments

Dear Jesus,

Compliments can be dangerous words that snag the soul. It's far too sweet to dwell on every enticing flattering syllable and forget Who's the Creator of every talent. Ego shrieks its insistent demand, how worthwhile am I! A little pride poison can lead to grave sin.

For what claim does the human person have to being grand? It's better to push compliments off the brink of memory and give sincere praise to God instead.

Jesus, You alone are worthy of all compliments and glory!

Exodus 15:2
The Lord is my strength and my defense; he has become my salvation. He is my God, and I will praise him, my father's God, and I will exalt him.

October 24

Heaven In Mind

Dear Jesus,

Occupy my mind with heaven, that I may accomplish much upon earth. Give me daily doses of heavenly hope. Let me not be so worldly fixated as to ignore my longing for what earth cannot give.

Every personal temporal desire I achieve soon loses its meaning. It seems in the acquisition and/or accomplishment to be over-rated. Serving as hands and hearts for others is often very hard, but deeply pleasurable both during and afterwards.

Keeping heaven in mind keeps me grounded and active here on earth.

Matthew 5:16
In the same way, let your light shine before others, that they may see your good deeds and glorify your Father in heaven.

Tension

Dear Jesus,

An undefined tension is seeping into my pores and unsettling my feelings. Thought clouds fill me with foreboding. Something is amiss, real or imagined, I don't know.

My heart goes on alert. Imaginings scatter like seeds. I try to gather them up. With effort and repetition I refocus on what is true, noble, right and good, and pure. I pray, Jesus, make holy this day. May Your peace and love permeate me. Meet my physical and spiritual needs and keep my heart pure from sin and guilt. Unleash Your power to deliver me from evil. May Your will be unstoppable on earth as it is in heaven.

Soon uneasiness flees. Thank You Jesus, peace reigns supreme again.

2 Chronicles 34:31
The king stood by His pillar and renewed the covenant in the presence of the Lord—to follow the Lord and keep His commands, statutes and decrees with all His heart and all His soul, and to obey the words of the covenant written in this book.

October 26

Life Moments

Dear Jesus,

I fail, I call on You, I mourn, I rise. I cry, I smile. I need, I receive. I give, I have. All these life moments are possible because I love You above all that is, or was, or will be.

You've let me loose in the world to love or to hate, to run and avoid or to go and serve. I'm set loose to wound and destroy or build and heal. I can be a surface see-er and a surface seek-er or go deep with You and serve Your people faithfully during the moments of my life.

I choose to be, Jesus, whatever You want me to be and do. You're the Lord of heaven and earth Who never fails me.

Psalm 30:5
For His anger lasts only a moment, but His favor lasts a lifetime; weeping may stay for the night, but rejoicing comes in the morning.

October 27

Holy Music

Dear Jesus,

I make music in my head and heart unto You. I cannot keep from it. I sing a litany of gratitude. I'm overcome with splendor and surprise at the way You care for my body and my soul.

I ponder this gift of uplifting music. It glorifies You and inspires thoughts of infinity, making ripples of spiritual passion explode within me.

Is it because music is Your sound permeating the universe? Praise You, Jesus, for giving me ears and heart to hear the music. It becomes my own beautiful melody exalting You.

2 Chronicles 29:28
The whole assembly bowed in worship, while the musicians played and the trumpets sounded. All this continued until the sacrifice of the burnt offering was completed.

October 28

Prayer Tool

Dear Jesus,

Prayer is an amazing tool. It's functional, comforting, and exciting. Prayer doesn't take my time, it enriches it. Prayer doesn't consume my energy, it expands it. Prayer is a tool that's always sharp and always effective.

May I pray for every concern You put on my heart. Let it be my go-to default mode. I want to be a prayer warrior for those You've placed within my sphere of care and given me to love.

Guide me when You want me to add specific action to my praying.

I'll obey You in every detail. May I meet every need You ask me to fill through using my prayer tool and performing deeds for Your glory.

1 Kings 8:54
When Solomon had finished all these prayers and supplications to the Lord, he rose from before the altar of the Lord, where he had been kneeling with His hands spread out toward heaven.

October 29

The Wait

Dear Jesus,

I've observed a suffering person and beseeched You for a miracle. Yet no results are visible. The painful wait is taking its toll. I can only imagine the impact on this soul. Certainly, Your Divine ears have heard. Jesus, what are You about in this situation?

Allowing such human suffering seems absurd, You're the epitome of kindness and love. There must be a purpose larger than I know. Trust is required, yet it's so hard. But I do.

I resolve to pray and praise and reject doubt. Speedily, may Your will be accomplished as I wait. I trust that You are good always.

1 Peter 5:10
But after you have suffered for a little while, the God of all grace, who calls you to share His eternal glory in union with Christ, will himself perfect you and give you firmness, strength, and a sure foundation.

October 30

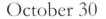

Wealth

Dear Jesus,

Many people are on the hunt for material treasure, using maps that disintegrate in their unfolding. How can gold and gems satisfy without riches for the soul?

While seeking fragile treasure troves, sparkling, illusory jewels, golden chests, void of lasting joy, many of Your people perish. Joy is found within the realm of the Triune God where true wealth abounds. It's within the human spirit that You deposit pearls of precious truth.

Jesus, wealth is seeking Your wisdom and walking in Your will. It's traveling along Your biblical road map of goodness and grace.

1 Timothy 6:17
Command those who are rich in this present world not to be arrogant nor to put their hope in wealth, which is so uncertain, but to put their hope in God, who richly provides us with everything for our enjoyment.

October 31

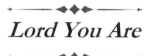

Lord You Are

Dear Jesus,

I watch with awe as You burst a new day into existence. Morning charges out of night with a streaming sun. Nature's sounds intensify as these new twenty-four hours spring from Your hand.

As my eyes absorb the dawn I'm reminded again that You're the joy that incites my smile. You're the glow that lights my soul. You're the fire that ignites my brain and the peace that prompts my rest. You're the source of meaning in my life and my beloved who whispers words of love. Jesus, have I told You lately that You're all this and more to me every day?

You supernaturally touch my heart. I feel Your presence and absorb Your beauty as I welcome this new day.

Psalm 116

I love the Lord, because … He listens to me every time I call to him. The danger of death was all around me; the horrors of the grave closed in on me; I was filled with fear and anxiety. Then I called to the Lord, "I beg you, Lord, save me!" The Lord is merciful and good; our God is compassionate. The Lord protects the helpless; when I was in danger, he saved me.

November 1

It's Time

Dear Jesus,

In the middle of the night, my mind awakens. My soul needs to speak to You, my ever-present Lord. You await me.

It's time for our sharing.
It's time for hearing Your truth.
It's time for feeling Your love.
It's time for appreciating Your goodness.
It's time for experiencing Your gentleness.
It's time for hearing Your orders.
It's time for engaging in Your worship.
It's always Jesus time.
Always.

Ecclesiastes 3:16-17
He has made everything beautiful in its time. He has also set eternity in the human heart; yet no one can fathom what God has done from beginning to end. I said to myself, "God will bring into judgment both the righteous and the wicked, for there will be a time for every activity, a time to judge every deed.

November 2

Lethargy

Dear Jesus,

I'm feeling low. Please make my lethargy go away. Breathe life into my 206 bones. Restore my millions of brain cells. Energize my 600 muscles. Refresh my non-stopping heart and lungs. Cleanse my marvelous organs.

Thinking about the word "triumph" encourages me. The spelling is simply tri- with the "umph" added. Jesus, I need to try and You're the source of all "umph." I'm counting on Your "umph" today. No devil, world, or fleshly foe can keep me low.

Please shore me up today as Joshua and Aaron held up the arms of Moses when they became tired during battle. This support ultimately assured a victory. Refresh my body please. I have a busy schedule today. May I surge through it for Your glory.

Psalm 69:16-18
Answer me, Lord, out of the goodness of your love; in your great mercy turn to me. Do not hide your face from your servant; answer me quickly, for I am in trouble. Come near and rescue me; deliver me because of my foes.

November 3

Transgressions

Dear Jesus,

Jesus, my occasional selfish and aggressive demeanor is dangerous. Guard me from it. I long to have a new heart and spirit, one that doesn't transgress. Transgression means to "gress" or go across, aggression means to "gress" or go against. Both behaviors revolt against established limits and lack graciousness. For my transgressions, Jesus, You were crucified.

I make the Gospels my model for serving You and Your people. May my heart and home be a holy place where people feel safe.

Grace me with a sweet, determined spirit – not an obnoxious demeanor. Balance me with Your love because I represent You wherever I go.

Ezekiel 18:31
Rid yourselves of all the offenses you have committed, and get a new heart and a new spirit. Why will you die, people of Israel?

November 4

Perfect

Dear Jesus,

You're the only perfect Person Who ever was or will be. Your help is always present and perfect. Yours is the strength that never fails, the love that will not diminish.

Your care for me is thorough and precise. You consider all my plans and filter them through Your wisdom. Thank you, beloved Jesus for being completely dependable.

You're the One who gives me divine wake up calls when Your nudges stir me from sleep. I delight in our night visits. When You speak I'm eager to listen. Day or night Lord You guide me and love me perfectly.

Proverbs !:5
…let the wise listen and add to their learning, and let the discerning get guidance—

November 5

Soul Stirring

Dear Jesus,

Jesus, stir my soul with passion for those lost souls who live as if dead, dabbling in empty pursuits for pleasure.

Make me bold and eager to speak of Your reality. Do with me what needs doing so I'll be selfless and courageous, even if it results in my feeling pain and rejection. Help me be well prepared as a truth-speaker. Guide my study and strengthen me.

You've given me the privilege of being a messenger of Your salvation. Empower me to stir the souls of those who need to know about Your incredible sacrifice and love.

Philippians 1:9
And this is my prayer: that your love may abound more and more in knowledge and depth of insight, so that you may be able to discern what is best and may be pure and blameless for the day of Christ, filled with the fruit of righteousness that comes through Jesus Christ—to the glory and praise of God.

November 6

"Oh Jesus"

Dear Jesus,

I'm not a singer, but You gave me a passionate song. I'm not a speaker, but You made me a divine orator. I'm not a dancer, but oh You make me twirl with joy. I'm not a giver, but You've made me a generous servant. I'm not a people person, but You made me passionate for souls.

I watch You light up my life like a bolt of lightning. Other times You work with a quiet breeze of movement. Always You exert tender power.

I breathe out "Oh, Jesus," my favorite prayer - these two small words make me shiver with emotion. To speak them makes my soul soar. "Oh, Jesus."

Ephesians 3:19
...and to know this love that surpasses knowledge—that you may be filled to the measure of all the fullness of God.

November 7

Self-striving

Dear Jesus,

The end of the world as described in the book of Revelation draws closer day by day. Knowledge without wisdom abounds. Demons of deceit swarm everywhere. Devils of destruction attack families. Disasters multiply upon the earth as You well know.

All the while human striving and whining over trifles continues. Does this ceaseless selfishness disappoint You? I marvel at how strong Your patience is as You deal with human beings and watch the future unfold.

At the same time Your faithful followers shun self-focus and prepare for Your glorious reappearance with eager expectation. I'm excited to be among them. Come Lord Jesus.

Revelation 21: 7-8
Those who are victorious will inherit all this, and I will be their God and they will be my children. But the cowardly, the unbelieving, the vile, the murderers, the sexually immoral, those who practice magic arts, the idolaters and all liars—they will be consigned to the fiery lake of burning sulfur. This is the second death."

November 8

Sustained

Dear Jesus,

The world startles me at times with its many temptations.

I love that You take me deep into a place of safety. Help me to the place of purity away from flurries of sinful thoughts fluttering in my mind. Sacred and pure, You protect me. Encircling, embracing, and enfolding me with Your love and wisdom.

Sift through all that encumbers me. Shake away my temptations to be vengeful and unkind. May my heart be sustained with Your goodness and peace.

Titus 3:3
At one time we too were foolish, disobedient, deceived and enslaved by all kinds of passions and pleasures. We lived in malice and envy, being hated and hating one another.

November 9

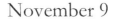

Heavenly Life

Dear Jesus,

Life in heaven – what will it be like? I hear stories of glistening natural beauty and colors never before seen. Will there be glorious glimpses of new realities? Trillions of ideas bursting simultaneously into existence? A precious never before experienced sense of completion? Human beings turned into living jewels of perfection?

I love to imagine life in Your presence, the source of all that is. Intimate contact with the Holy Spirit, energizer of all excites me beyond words! Already You filled me with compassion and empowered me with boldness on earth, what will power in heaven be like? How awesome to see evil shattered permanently and the Spirit soaring.

Face to face with You, Jesus, I'll be in awe beyond imagining. I visualize heaven to be all this and more.

Ephesians 1:3
Praise be to the God and Father of our Lord Jesus Christ, who has blessed us in the heavenly realms with every spiritual blessing in Christ.

November 10

Connecting

Dear Jesus,

I'm thrilled to guide others to encounter Your divine reality. What joy to evangelize and watch the Holy Spirit connect people to You. How exciting when a depressed soul becomes aware of the possibility of new life. The truth about You administered with solicitous love creates beautiful, faith-filled disciples.

Jesus, in accepting this holy task of connecting people I'm fully aware of my unworthiness. My lack of confidence surprisingly doesn't distress me because I depend on prayer power at every turn. You blast my fears away. I receive Your help. Nothing interrupts Your Spirit's flow.

Jesus, what a delight to watch when these connections lead to human transformation. How amazing to observe shriveled hearts refreshed with living water. Thank you for allowing me to participate in this work of Your Spirit.

Matthew 10:42
And if anyone gives even a cup of cold water to one of these little ones who is my disciple, truly I tell you, that person will certainly not lose their reward.

November 11

Pruning

Dear Jesus,

I need more pruning. I sense I've some unruly ends, perhaps a few shoots heading in the wrong direction. Will You prune me personally or choose another to cut and snip me?

What events will become my pruning situations? Ready for the shears, I'm braced for the pinching, pulling, and cuts that make me fuller and stronger and help me conform to Your commandments. I know Your principles are a gift, ordinances true and righteous, illuminating and instructive.

My great, loving Trimmer, Your nips reveal my lapses and errors, and prevent sin from having dominion over me. Keeping Your law and walking in Your will are my desire. Prune me well Jesus.

John 15:1-4
"I am the true vine, and my Father is the gardener. He cuts off every branch in me that bears no fruit, while every branch that does bear fruit he prunes so that it will be even more fruitful. You are already clean because of the word I have spoken to you. Remain in me, as I also remain in you. No branch can bear fruit by itself; it must remain in the vine.

November 12

Ever Deeper

Dear Jesus,

Wonder of wonders, You deign to invite me into Your presence. You encourage my efforts and dote on me. You've demonstrated countless times Your immense kindness, incredible self-sacrifice and patience. You exhibit supernatural love eons beyond the natural. Your deep holiness is beyond description.

Jesus, I want to go ever deeper in Your Word and become more like You. I long to be able to spread Your amazing love and act without selfish interests.

In all my ways I strive to imitate You. I hope to never disappoint You my beloved Jesus.

Exodus 34:10
Then the Lord said: "I am making a covenant with you. Before all your people I will do wonders never before done in any nation in all the world. The people you live among will see how awesome is the work that I, the Lord, will do for you.

November 13

Goodness

Dear Jesus,

The letters in the word godness are the same letters in godness minus one "o." How appropriate since goodness is personified in God. Total, true goodness exists nowhere else.

I can only imagine what it's like to do no wrong! To have all my ways always be just!

Jesus, I love this quality of goodness in You. I long to emulate Your goodness. Teach me how I may reflect one zillionith of Your intense goodness, the foundation of Your greatness.

Exodus 33:19

And the Lord said, "I will cause all my goodness to pass in front of you, and I will proclaim my name, the Lord, in your presence. I will have mercy on whom I will have mercy, and I will have compassion on whom I will have compassion.

November 14

Expectant Faith

Dear Jesus,

I believe in Your ability to transform even hideous events. Truthfully, I don't always like Your ways or timing, but I treasure Your will and the ultimate outcome. You have total wisdom.

Faith in You removes my what-if fears and sustains my peace. Faith determines my ability to live confidently despite this situation. I trust You whatever.

I may not feel Your love at this moment, but I believe in Your loving-kindness. I don't sense Your anointing on my life, but I recognize it exists. I don't see Your healing at work, but I believe in Your power to heal. I await with expectant faith Your solutions.

Deuteronomy 32: 3-4
I will proclaim the name of the Lord. Oh, praise the greatness of our God! He is the Rock, His works are perfect, and all His ways are just. A faithful God who does no wrong, upright and just is he.

November 15

Time Alone

Dear Jesus,

My life is occasionally like an unraveling ball. Sometimes the ends dangle every which way. I picture myself wrapping these ends around You, my solid core. This reconnection happens during my times of silence.

I love to be alone with You. Sometimes I revel in the simple reality of Your existence. I'm content to live an ordinary life made extraordinary by our relationship. What a joy to have my ongoing inner dialogue with You.

You tell me I can accomplish much when I venture into the world. After being fortified by time alone with You I won't unravel. I'm armed with Your grace and truth. So be it!

Psalm 27:4
One thing I ask from the Lord, this only do I seek: that I may dwell in the house of the Lord all the days of my life, to gaze on the beauty of the Lord and to seek him in His temple.

November 16

Flashes

Dear Jesus,

You say, I love you, precious child. Keep your mind and body alert and be available for my sparks. These will be like little flashes spurring you to action. My prompts will help you process the lessons in your circumstances and recognize what needs doing. Act in confidence, through my Spirit, filled with peace and purpose.

To my amazement You say that I'm baptized and anointed, and I'm Your beloved, the delight of Your eyes. You guide me daily for Your glory.

You tell me my life can be an Alleluia story. You want me to bring flashes of Your blessings to the world. What a privilege! Thank You for trusting each of us to do this.

Psalm 52:8
But I am like an olive tree flourishing in the house of God; I trust in God's unfailing love forever and ever.

November 17

Thoughts of You

Dear Jesus,

Thoughts of You casually enter my present moments, then become my major focus. This happens at multiple times like sunrise when I'm watching You light up the dark world, or being outdoors any time walking in the beautiful creation You designed.

In my seconds of stillness there is but one awareness: You're within me and all about me. How I treasure these interludes when all sound stops and I no longer sense my setting. Warmth and contentment fill me.

I'm in Your presence, where I long to stay always, My Jesus, my Lord above all.

Revelation 19:5-8
Praise our God, all you His servants, you who fear him, both great and small! Then I heard what sounded like a great multitude, like the roar of rushing waters and like loud peals of thunder, shouting: "Hallelujah! For our Lord God Almighty reigns. Let us rejoice and be glad and give him glory!"

November 18

The Thrill

Dear Jesus,

Words of praise flow from my heart. Faith in You removes all anxiety. I'm basking in knowledge of Your Presence. I have perfect peace focused on You.

Each morning the thrill comes again. I awake with exciting thoughts of You. Your love is present, powerful and permanent.

Jesus, You truly make me bold and complete. You've turned me into a well-equipped new creation.

2 Corinthians 5:17
Therefore, if anyone is in Christ, the new creation has come: The old has gone, the new is here!

November 19

Problem-solving

Dear Jesus,

I can be a master of denial and a mistress of forgetting. Often I have confidence about tomorrow, but sometimes I'm negligent in dealing with problems today. Help me appropriate the divine power I've received to handle problems that arise.

I need to ignore the urgent clamor around me so I won't miss Your answers for me.

Jesus with Your grace may I never disappoint You in my process of problem solving and people helping. I rely upon Your anointing.

1 John 2:27
As for you, the anointing you received from him remains in you, and you do not need anyone to teach you. But as His anointing teaches you about all things and as that anointing is real, not counterfeit—just as it has taught you, remain in him.

November 20

A Plea

Dear Jesus,

Hear my plea for my friend, I'm crying out, help her please. She's a lover of Your Word and Your ways and needs major healing. She trusts You, and often speaking of Your healing power boldly.

Heal this precious woman so that her voice may continue to be heard on earth. Please honor her sincere faith with nothing less than an outrageous miracle.

I pray fervently as well for her family enduring unspeakable pain as they watch her suffer. Praise You Jesus that Your compassionate healing continues in this day.

Jeremiah 33:6
Nevertheless, I will bring health and healing to it; I will heal my people and will let them enjoy abundant peace and security.

November 21

Heart Touching

Dear Jesus,

How intriguing are Your methods. You touch my heart with Your love, and empower me to touch other hearts. You graciously let me participate in Your process of heart touching!

Heart touching is always a movement of the Spirit. With Your invisible energy and Your amazing anointing, I'm capable of impacting countless minds and hearts.

My delight comes from being guided and used by You, my Life Designer. Jesus, please keep me productive through You and for You with Your heart touching power forever.

Psalm 44:10
I do not hide your righteousness in my heart; I speak of your faithfulness and your saving help. I do not conceal your love and your faithfulness from the great assembly.

November 22

Cooking

Dear Jesus,

It's intriguing to think of cooking terms in connection with your transformation of me. I picture you preparing my soul. You:

Marinate me with joy. Pepper me with patience. Salt me with compassion. Chop me for tenderness. Saturate me with peace. Coat me with kindness. Sear me with sensitivity. Heat me with holiness. Bake me in the oven of trial. Broil away my dross. May I be savory food for a hungry world.

This human preparation is necessary. Jesus, I treasure the incarnation of Your mystery that I'm to die to myself so You may fully live in me and make me a delicacy to bless others.

Galatians 5:22
But the fruit of the Spirit is love, joy, peace, forbearance, kindness, goodness, faithfulness, gentleness and self-control.

November 23

Magnificence

Dear Jesus,

Praise surges across my lips and I must sing and speak about You. You're the essence of all goodness, the instigator of every action and watchman of every human endeavor. Jesus, all this and more You are.

Your magnificence dwells in mystery. Once garbed in glory and majesty, You left heaven to dwell in flesh clothed with earthly garments to save humankind.

You fill my prayers with melody. I long to make holy songs on earth that will resound as music in heaven. You alone are worthy of every song of adoration sung. You give my soul the music it needs to hear. You are Jesus, only and eternal, deserving of endless praise.

Isaiah 42:10
Sing to the Lord a new song, His praise from the ends of the earth, you who go down to the sea, and all that is in it, you islands, and all who live in them.

November 24

Cherished

Dear Jesus,

To be cherished and guided by You is no small thing in a culture that frequently confuses facts and distorts reality. I've made self-centered choices based on surface allure and learned they only lead to future disappointments.

Jesus, may Your truth expose every disguise and deceit. You're the one reliable path of truth leading to lasting love and soul success.

You alone give me a meaningful life now and the promise of breath eternal. No one cherishes and guides like You.

Acts 17:25
And he is not served by human hands, as if he needed anything. Rather, he himself gives everyone life and breath and everything else.

November 25

Invisible Power

Dear Jesus,

Your Word tells me to engage in prayer non-stop. Prayer is human compassion charged by the divine power of God.

Invisible supernatural activity is instigated by prayer, the greatest power on earth. Spiritual power is intensified after a period of intense prayer. Prayer requires stick-to-it-ness and is so worthwhile.

With confidence I pray huge, mighty prayers for the needs of Your people. Jesus, I praise You for this amazing gift of prayer. I bow my head before You to get my divine orders throughout the day.

Romans 12:12
Be joyful in hope, patient in affliction, faithful in prayer.

November 26

Daily Blessings

Dear Jesus,

I love every small daily blessing: the greeting of a loved one, the cheery presence of a co-worker, the fragrance of nature, enthusiasm for work I enjoy, and joyful satisfaction from my efforts. My greatest blessing however is an awareness of You throughout my day.

How amazing that You, totally divine, entered the sphere of time, clothed as a baby, imbued with eternity, and shattered the barrier between God and man so that I might experience daily blessings.

Freedom became available to all humanity. Sin's darkness encountered Living Light and joy unspeakable is now my legacy. Praise You Jesus for daily blessings.

Isaiah 45:3
I will give you hidden treasures, riches stored in secret places, so that you may know that I am the Lord, the God of Israel, who summons you by name.

November 27

Praise

Dear Jesus,

Your Word tells me "In all things give thanks." All? Really? During times of intense emotional and spiritual pain expressing praise is hard, if not nearly impossible. Where does such praise come from?

Perhaps this praise originates in the tiny heart place filled with faith that enlarges bit by bit through knowledge of the words in Scripture. It grows from a history of having seen You work trying human situations for good. It flows from the comfort of people who speak about Your presence and have confidence in Your ability to create an ultimate tapestry of beauty from each life.

Praising You before I see a good result can be difficult. I dislike every horrible event or sorrow, but love Your actions in dire circumstances to rescue or comfort me. Praise is sometimes hard, yes, but necessary within me. I counter the impact of fear or disbelief every time I express my praise.

1 Chronicles 16:36
Praise be to the Lord, the God of Israel, from everlasting to everlasting. Then all the people said "Amen" and "Praise the Lord."

November 28

War

Dear Jesus,

I try to exhibit Christlikeness but often I flop. How hurtful Jesus. You watch me and wait. You remind me of the dignity of effort and encourage me to try again. Unseen forces battle against me in this war that began in Eden.

Spiritual growth is from You Lord. Power to forgive despite gouges of emotional pain. The ability to receive forgiveness that's undeserved. Power to burn brightly when I'd like to hide. You urge me to love when the enemy inspires me to hate. You lift me from the pits of petulance and pity.

Help also comes to me from others who love You. Encouraged by them, I emerge. Jesus, You always know who I am, how I am, whose I am, and what I shall be. Your team, our team, succeeds ultimately. Hallelujah.

Psalm 31:9, 14-15

Be merciful to me, Lord, for I am in distress; my eyes grow weak with sorrow, my soul and body with grief. But I trust in you, Lord; I say, You are my God. My times are in your hands; deliver me from the hands of my enemies, from those who pursue me.

November 29

Paul and Peter

❖❖❖

Dear Jesus,

I'm inspired by Paul's presence in Scriptures by his fervor and fire. I admire his obsession for advancing Your kingdom. I understand his passion for retelling the good news of salvation and his disregard for personal safety. I'm impressed by his acceptance of a painful, permanent thorn of flesh and his persistence despite opposition. Paul's life encourages my determination.

I'm also inspired by Peter's presence in Scripture. His personality is so like mine. Expediency often overruled his wise judgment. His impulsiveness was huge. A liar, he was transformed into a speaker of truth. His inner strength and courage became solid as rock. Peter realized salvation came only through You. Peter's life inspires my perseverance.

Paul and Peter are both great role models for me in living out my Christian life. Thank You Jesus for them.

Acts 4:12-13
When they saw the courage of Peter and John[and Paul] and realized that they were unschooled, ordinary men, they were astonished and they took note that these men had been with Jesus.

November 30

Decision

Dear Jesus,

The age-old dilemma of humans is the choice to go our own way or accept Your plan of life. Rejection of You Jesus versus submission to Your will? Fulfill earthly desires or seek eternal satisfaction? Shall I be the Master of my life or You? Worship You or the world?

The choice is also between being depressed, frightened, insecure, and confused or being purpose-filled, joyful, and secure. These qualities come through access to Your Holy Spirit's peace and wisdom. The choice is to stay the same or come and be changed by You, the One Who alone has power to transform, save, and heal. You're the real living Lord.

I've made my choice and I'm never changing my mind - Your way Jesus forever.

Deuteronomy 30:19
This day I call the heavens and the earth as witnesses against you that I have set before you life and death, blessings and curses. Now choose life, so that you and your children may live.

December 1

Feelings

Dear Jesus,

I sense You encourage me to be aware of my feelings and identify their source. You don't want me to deny or reject my feelings, but neither should I be controlled by them.

How different! When I was young I often heard "Stop feeling like that, don't cry, don't show my anger, someone might see." I concluded that feelings were bad and should be squelched. Jesus, You've showed me feelings are a strong and good part of me. I'm made in Your image and You feel deeply. Your Word has taught me to rejoice in being a feeling human being as well as a thinking human. Both thoughts and feelings are intertwined by You to further Your plan for my life.

Although feelings are normal and natural, they're not to be primary motives for my decisions. I must control my emotions wisely.

Titus 2:11-12
For the grace of God…teaches us to say "No" to ungodliness and worldly passions, and to live self-controlled, upright and godly lives in this present age.

December 2

Sound of Sin

Dear Jesus,

Does sin have a sound? If so, what might it be like? An ugly cacophonous reverberation?

Or maybe like a thousand sheets of breaking glass? A stampede of raging elephants? A hurricane assaulting the earth?

If sin does make a noise, Jesus, I don't want to hear it. Help me avoid activating it through my continual fidelity to You.

Matthew 9:13
But go and learn what this means: 'I desire mercy, not sacrifice.' For I have not come to call the righteous, but sinners."

December 3

◆◆◆

Fascinating Words

◆◆◆

Dear Jesus,

Reading Your Word I smile, cry, laugh and shake my head. Sometimes I reel with shock. I mean Ezekiel? Hosea? Song of Solomon? What mazing life stories I ponder as I study. You say don't judge non-believers, but to a Christian brother or sister in sin lovingly point out wrongdoing that deviates from Scripture.

What a privilege to apply the fascinating principles in Your Word. Who could understand Scripture without the Holy Spirit's help?

Jesus, I long for all to know the value inherent in studying Your direct revelation to us through Your Word. How much easier our life story becomes with it.

Deuteronomy 31:12
Assemble the people—men, women and children, and the foreigners residing in your towns—so they can listen and learn to fear the Lord your God and follow carefully all the words of this law.

December 4

Time

Dear Jesus,

You established the concept of time. I watch it move past. I fill it and try to stretch it. Often I need more than I have.

The events of every twenty-four hours can hold surprises. Some are welcome, others shocking. The demands of time require constant action and adjustment throughout my day.

I like it best when You control my time. You guide me through my days with a smooth flow not my own. Some day, You will stop time altogether. Until then, Master of All Time, direct me in the use of mine, moment by moment.

2 Corinthians 6:2
For he says, "In the time of my favor I heard you, and in the day of salvation I helped you." I tell you, now is the time of God's favor, now is the day of salvation.

December 5

World Walker

Dear Jesus,

After thirty years of average, common, unremarkable living on earth, You became a shocking, controversial, world-changing mover and shaker.

Your exploded into society, breaking the norms, shattering Jewish theology and remaking human lives. Jesus, what a God-man, what a Life-Changer, what a Savior!

I walk through the world You made with my head high, heart bowed and mind humbled. I'm heaven bound because of You and I enjoy gifts undeserved. I'm prepared to suffer if necessary to defend Your truth. I live in Your presence and with Your power. I move among an army of Christian world-walkers ready to shake the world for Your glory.

Hebrews 5:7-8
During the days of Jesus' life on earth, He offered up prayers and petitions with fervent cries and tears to the one who could save Him from death, and He was heard because of His reverent submission. Son though He was, He learned obedience from what He suffered.

December 6

Each Day

Dear Jesus,

In heaven will there be a library with files for all our days? I picture walking over to a shelf and picking one out, perhaps today, reliving it in my mind and knowing how it felt to be alive this day – its atmosphere, emotional tone, degree of sun and shadow.

Not just each twenty-four hours but all of life is ever-changing daily, flowing toward perfection in You. No wonder each day is precious in Your sight.

May I use my time well – fill it with wholesome thoughts, words and actions. You've determined my present space. My impact isn't measured in size, nor scored by points. I'm to live with grace each day wherever You place me.

Ecclesiastes 8:5
Whoever obeys His command will come to no harm, and the wise heart will know the proper time and procedure.

December 7

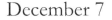

Burnings

Dear Jesus,

I walked into one of life's burnings today and entered the dynamic of another family's pain. I attempted to bring love and unity.

In the process I got singed with Satan's firepower. Help me recover, Jesus. Seal my skin with holy ointment. Refresh my mind, heart and soul. I'm drained, depleted. You alone are my heart-healer. You alone are my soul-shield. You are truly my God beyond compare.

Diminish my desire to withdraw when presented with difficult situations. Jesus, comfort me, revive my smoldering ashes that I may pray wisely and serve these people again. I name them in Your Presence and place them before You for protection and guidance. I'm totally trusting them to You, yet willing to do my part. Only by focusing on You can I endure life's burnings.

Psalm 143:7-8
Answer me quickly, Lord; my spirit fails. Do not hide Your face from me or I will be like those who go down to the pit. Let the morning bring me word of Your unfailing love, for I have put my trust in You. Show me the way I should go, for to You I entrust my life.

December 8

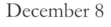

Friends

Dear Jesus,

Some friends drop into my life lightly like raindrops appearing out of nowhere. Others arrive like lightning bolts.

Some friends are golden oldies, others new, a few quickly become permanent treasures, and others stay only short term. Each fits into a different slot, these people You've given me as friends. Some need my assistance, a few stretch me as we contend. Many inspire me to new pursuits, and bless me no end. Needy or renewing, all my friends ultimately enrich my life.

I watch, Jesus, as You flip my relationships about, bringing in, taking out, these amazing people You've put into my life.

Philippians 4:1
Therefore, my brothers and sisters, you whom I love and long for, my joy and crown, stand firm in the Lord in this way, dear friends!

December 9

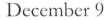

Yield

Dear Jesus,

I used to yield readily to the opinion of others. I assumed their thoughts were more significant and automatically conceded their thoughts were right. Now I only yield to Your wisdom. I'm blessed to exercise discernment through Your Spirit. Then I express myself using holy authority and knowledge.

I'm fortified through Your amazing Spirit, ever-present and available to me.

I don't need the agreement of others if I have Your approval, Jesus. I feel fearless at all times now. Living this way is so freeing. How I appreciate You.

Isaiah 48:11
For My own sake, for My own sake, I do this. How can I let Myself be defamed? I will not yield My glory to another.

Holy Shine

Dear Jesus,

Give me a holy shine, inside and out. I want to be a light-giver reflecting Your image. Only Your brightness gives me clarity.

Shine Your light before me, shine it within me. I need Your light to penetrate my being. Without Your light I can easily get clouded.

I long to glitter and sparkle for You.

1 Corinthians 4:5
Therefore judge nothing before the appointed time; wait until the Lord comes. He will bring to light what is hidden in darkness and will expose the motives of the heart. At that time each will receive their praise from God.

December 11

Piercing Darts

Dear Jesus,

Why do I grieve? Why indeed? You made me in Your image and sometimes life seems unfair. Situations hurt and disappoint me, Jesus. You tasted life's putridness and bitterness. I don't expect fairness, but my heart longs for it. I easily slip into ego spins: I should be treated well, spoken of highly, and never ignored.

Darts of selfishness pierce me. Humility disappears and pride reigns until You re-balance me, Jesus. I find joy again in daily activity as a blessing speaker and a harmony bringer. I can be peace-filled and joyful whatever my circumstances by Your grace.

Faith is quite simple really. It's total trust in Your great power, unsurpassable wisdom, and all-encompassing goodness. Jesus, from Your Word, I know Your justice will prevail one day. Until then, You alone will be my primary happiness.

2 Corinthians 7:11
See what this godly sorrow has produced in you: what earnestness, what eagerness to clear yourselves, what indignation, what alarm, what longing, what concern, what readiness to see justice done. At every point you have proved yourselves to be innocent in this matter.

December 12

Loved and Hated

Dear Jesus,

I love You for Your exquisite compassion, Your thought-provoking wisdom, and sin-breaking power.

Many hate You for Your unequivocal message of love. You disturbed the status quo, and insisted on worship of one God, three in one, Father, Son and Spirit. Love and hatred surrounded You when You walked the earth. You still innocently provoke people today.

Loved and hated, wisely, boldly and fearlessly You taught. May I speak like You diligently with zeal. It's actually quite a thrill to be honored, loved and hated as You are.

Mark 13:13
Everyone will hate you because of Me, but the one who stands firm to the end will be saved.

December 13

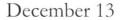

Weary

Dear Jesus,

I awake weary. Jesus, I need Your energy. Mine isn't sufficient for today. Every movement is an effort. I'm squeezed dry.

Pain threatens me, tempting me to succumb to inactivity and urges me to step back. Jesus, please renew me. Make me fresh.

May I display my faith well today. Carve it into my soul, Jesus. I long to display fruit for You. Your divine plan is always worth doing.

Psalm 119:28
My soul is weary with sorrow; strengthen me according to Your word.

December 14

God's Dialogue

Dear Jesus,

You're such an amazing communicator. Angels hear, waves roar, mountains disappear.

Your voice Jesus, is what I listen for. Only Yours will do. Speak to me. Like Samuel of old I am your servant awaiting communication. Life's frenzy is loud - I refuse to allow it to drown You out.

Perhaps I'll hear You today in the wind. Or the words of a friend. Perhaps You'll speak through the ancient Biblical Word known for thousands of years. I sense the intersection of heaven and earth happens when You speak and I hear.

Psalm 16:7-9
I will praise the Lord, who counsels me; even at night my heart instructs me. I keep my eyes always on the Lord. With Him at my right hand, I will not be shaken. Therefore my heart is glad and my tongue rejoices; my body also will rest secure.

December 15

Where

Dear Jesus,

Where is the body of Christ today? We're meant to be
Your visible sign in the world now.

Where is the mind of Christ?
We're empowered to be Your wisdom among men
and women.

Where are the apostles of Christ?
We're meant to speak Your good news.

Where are Christ's warriors for justice?
We're created to be standard-bearers of Your truth.

Where are the faith-filled believers performing
wonders?
Where are Your people, Jesus?

Where am I?

1 Corinthians 12:27
Now you are the body of Christ, and each one of you is a part of it.

December 16

Marvelous

Dear Jesus,

You're the God of action and accomplishment. You're also the God of no-hurry - I can reject scurry and flurry because You're the God of peace and contentment. No need to waste my life with tension and strife. How marvelous!

You're also God of the unexpecteds. You've shown me Jesus, how these unexpecteds often open doors to positive aspects of life. Aspects that would never have been experienced otherwise. Jesus I praise You for every unexpected and all those yet to come. Nothing is unexpected to You.

I can trust in You completely. You've promised to give me confidence for life's challenges and rest in the midst of them. How great is this!

Proverbs 4:4
Then he taught me, and he said to me, "Take hold of my words with all your heart; keep my commands, and you will live."

December 17

Gift of Confessing

Dear Jesus,

I love the gift of confessing. It's freeing and motivates me to strive to do better. Forgive me, for I have sinned…

Every time I didn't extend Your love.
Every time I surrendered my joy.
Every time I made someone else's stress my own.
Every time I succumbed to fear of human beings.
Every time I considered myself self-sufficient.
Every time I neglected our relationship.
Every time I slipped into worry.
Every time I slipped into discontent.
Every time I forgot You created me to be magnificent.
Every time I doubted You would equip me.
Every time I didn't trust Your way.

Thank you Father for forgiving me, absolving my debt and re-purposing me with Your grace.

Nehemiah 9:3
They stood where they were and read from the Book of the Law of the Lord their God for a quarter of the day, and spent another quarter in confession and in worshiping the Lord their God.

December 18

Naysayers

Dear Jesus,

You often encountered negative people when You walked the earth. I hear them too – the naysayers. How nice to have Your example in interacting with them. Naysayers told You in effect "You can't do this or that, that's contrary to our man-made law and not how we do things." You ignored them. Always You focused on being about Your Father's business.

I mustn't be deterred by those around me who are negative and do and say little of value.

I can disregard the naysayers, the discouragers. My intent is to please You alone and choose my actions for Your approval. It matters not if I'm told our culture doesn't like an aspect of Your truth You've given me to share. I still must act and speak boldly with love.

Psalm 32:8
I will instruct you and teach you in the way you should go; I will counsel you with My loving eye on you.

December 19

My King

Dear Jesus,

Praise You, Jesus. Dispenser of Mercy. Giver of Favor. Reliever of Affliction. Fortress of Strength. Beacon of Wisdom. Refuge of My Soul. What a blessing to serve You. How precious You are. You don't separate secular and sacred. Everything is holy wherever you are present and You are present everywhere.

You met Moses outdoors at a burning bush. You healed sick people along the side of the road. You did ministry and teaching on earth both in the Temple and while You walked the roads around Jerusalem.

You speak to me and teach me when I'm outdoors in Your amazing world and when I sit with other believers within the walls of a church. Gratefully I sense Your presence. Joyfully, I fulfill Your commands. You have my eternal loyalty. No wonder I call You my King and serve You faithfully.

1 Timothy 1:17
Now to the King eternal, immortal, invisible, the only God, be honor and glory forever and ever. Amen.

December 20

Disappoint

Dear Jesus,

You never disappoint me. Disappoint is a sad sounding word. It implies something desired didn't happen. I've learned to withhold judgment when my expectation isn't immediately met. Often there's a blessing being slowly birthed. I'm glad You've give me eyes to see that what seems disappointing initially, is beautiful and precise when worked through Your hand.

I know You're the never-disappointing supreme Creator of every experience of value in my life. I used to think I wanted every detail of my existence to be my way. Now I know it's Your way I desire.

Because of You I can feel relaxed, confident and bold. I'm immersed in the care of the Father and directed through Your indwelling Holy Spirit. You never disappoint me.

Isaiah 49:23
Kings will be your foster fathers, and their queens your nursing mothers. They will bow down before you with their faces to the ground; they will lick the dust at your feet. Then you will know that I am the Lord; those who hope in Me will not be disappointed.

December 21

The Gift of Intellect

Dear Jesus,

Living in the world involves being exposed to its intellectual culture. Not being of the world is hard. Still I can avoid anything that's anti-good and anti-God. You call me to use my gift of intellect well, Jesus. You encourage me to evaluate and think carefully.

My mind is stretched, filled and constantly expanding in knowledge. The brain is designed to feast on facts and digest them. Knowledge is insufficient without Your wisdom.

May I use my intellect well for Your glory.

Proverbs 6:23
For this command is a lamp, this teaching is a light, and correction and instruction are the way to life.

December 22

The Unseen Real

Dear Jesus,

I've learned that the real that is unseen is more real than that which is seen. Your sustaining power, unobservable, untouchable permeates each atom, fusing the past with the present and future.

Jesus, You alone are without equal or effective opposition. You're the reality undergirding all.

Without You nothing would exist, through You all things were created. You humbly move among us still modeling a love such as the world has never seen before.

Colossians 1:15-18
The Son is the image of the invisible God, the firstborn over all creation. For in Him all things were created: things in heaven and on earth, visible and invisible, whether thrones or powers or rulers or authorities; all things have been created through Him and for Him.

December 23

Grace

Dear Jesus,

Your grace truly is amazing. Your supernatural power works within me motivating me and enabling me to do what's right and good. Grace empowers me and urges me forward or puts stops on my behavior. My words and deeds are selected using spiritual wisdom and accomplished by Your Spirit's enablement.

Grace is in the realm of mystery. I only know it's what makes possible living in the Spirit and pleasing You with my choices.

And it's a fun way to live! Expressing grace and mercy to others. Striving is unnecessary. I can relax and live my best in and through You, not alone, but in our grace connection.

Psalm 5:11-12
But let all those rejoice who put their trust in You; let them ever shout for joy, because You defend them let those also who love Your name be joyful in You. For You, O Jesus, will bless the righteous; with favor You will surround him as with a shield.

December 24

Resisting

Dear Jesus,

For supernatural challenges, I need Your Spirit-assistance please. Satan must flee. I won't be his host. I'm resisting with all my might this devil dancing in my mind, twirling me this way and that, distorting my desires, and scattering my thoughts. Help me I pray. Infuse me with Your strength.

And You do. How incredible that I can have divine communication bringing my need for protection and protection for others to You. What a privilege! I marvel at this mystery. When I resist the devil he must flee.

Your cross carrying amazes me too and your defeat of Satan's power by it. What an incredible sacrifice. I'm breathless at the work of Your Holy Spirit for me.

James 4:7
Therefore submit to God. Resist the devil and he will flee from you.

December 25

Christmas

Dear Jesus,

Gift-giving and parties are fun but many people enjoy the holiday without appreciating You. They're okay with following a star to You as the babe in Bethlehem, shepherds and wise men. However, they're not enthusiastic about a Savior growing up, dying and rising to release them from their bondage to sinfulness.

You emphasized the need for forgiveness. Many insisted then, and still do now, that they're sin free – the ultimate deception. Nor were You popular among church leaders who abused their authority and subjugated others, as some still do.

May all those who need to repent admit their need for a Savior and find release and joy. This is the sacred meaning of this Christmas season. I celebrate with all those who know the real reason for Your entrance into human history.

Psalm 62:5-8
Yes, my soul, find rest in God; my hope comes from Him. Truly He is my rock and my salvation; He is my fortress, I will not be shaken. My salvation and my honor depend on God; He is my mighty rock, my refuge. Trust in Him at all times, you people; pour out your hearts to Him, for God is our refuge.

December 26

Mary, Mother

Dear Jesus,

Your mother Mary is so fascinating. She's holiness undefinable and sweetness personified. A model of dignity she boldly instigated Your miracle of water changing into wine. She knew You well Jesus and was certain You'd help.

I like to picture Mary as a mom like me. Did she ever worry about You being raised properly? Or if Joseph would get enough carpentry jobs to support the family? Perhaps she never worried about anything after all she went through regarding your miraculous birth?

How awesome to have Mary as my spiritual Mother. This precious woman is truly an inspiration worthy of honor and respect.

Matthew 2:11
On coming to the house, they saw the child with His mother Mary, and they bowed down and worshiped Him. Then they opened their treasures and presented Him with gifts of gold, frankincense and myrrh.

December 27

Mercy

Dear Jesus,

It's easy to be sensitive to the failings of others because I recognize my own weaknesses. I'm grateful for Your mercy that restores me gently and speaks kindly, always with love. Your mercy spurns judgment, understands sin and helps me embrace other sinners.

The quality of mercy enables me to love others as You would. Human energy alone is insufficient. Occasionally I'm the brunt of attack. Sometimes I'd like to run and hide - being a recluse seems appealing when I'm drained. Yet You bid me to remain present for others pouring out mercy and comfort even when it's hard. Only Your supernatural power helps me.

Living in Your love, speaking of You, and ministering to others is my great delight. I long for all to know You as I do. What joy to see people respond to Your gracious mercy. Jesus, make me merciful, as You are merciful.

Isaiah 63:9
In all their distress He too was distressed, and the angel of His presence saved them. In His love and mercy He redeemed them; He lifted them up and carried them all the days of old.

December 28

Halos

Dear Jesus,

Real halos are pure, invisible and strong. Those who wear halos never see them at all. True halos stretch. They're made of elastic bands of love. Halos worn loosely stay on well.

Self-made halos on pseudo saints are hideous. Pressed on too tightly they offend both sinners and saints. They push away the individuals they presume to serve.

Jesus, may real halos multiply by millions. I see these holy halo crowns on splendid saints living now. I visualize seeing billions in heaven one day.

James 1:12
Blessed is the man that endureth temptation: for when he is tried, he shall receive the crown of life, which the Lord hath promised to them that love Him.

December 29

Saul's Call

Dear Jesus,

A Spirit-changed person is different. A "God-with-her or him" person is divinely directed. Saul was such a man for a time. Sadly he strayed from the way he'd been shown and the closeness he'd known.

What happened? Did his flesh tempt him with false insecurity despite Your anointing? Did Saul begin to think of his power as his own? Did he forget Your call? He certainly neglected to live it out.

We are all guardians of our inheritance from You, Jesus. Help me avoid such a fall.

1 Samuel 10:6-7
The Spirit of the Lord will come powerfully upon you, and you will prophesy with them; and you will be changed into a different person. Once these signs are fulfilled, do whatever your hand finds to do, for God is with you.

December 30

Travel For God

Dear Jesus,

Israel's holy judge, Samuel, traveled a circuit from Bethel to Gilgal to Mizpah yearly. Jair's thirty sons rode thirty donkeys and controlled thirty towns as leaders of Israel for twenty-two years. Paul was also a busy traveling man.

I'm a traveler within my geographical area for You. Nothing can keep me bound. I'm called to be a disciple unto the nations starting with my neighborhood.

How shall I accomplish this? One act of love upon another. One touch of kindness, one precious word of comfort, one encouraging exhortation.

1 Samuel 7:15-17
Samuel continued as Israel's leader all the days of his life. From year to year he went on a circuit from Bethel to Gilgal to Mizpah, judging Israel in all those places. But he always went back to Ramah, where his home was, and there he also held court for Israel.

December 31

God's Plan

Dear Jesus,

You're our Life-Designer and Forever-Flawless-God. You've made an exquisite world. Your life plan for humans is precise with appointed times for birth and death. You're in control of all beginnings and endings on earth.

Someday death will reach me, perhaps with pain, but ultimately it will lead me to the joy of Your presence. How similar to birth, where a process of maternal pain, led me into this exquisite world.

I'm wondering what it will be like Jesus, the actual moment of ending my time on earth. I'll make an instantaneous shift from what's here to life beyond. The ever new, ageless experience of eternity sounds enchanting. How will I feel when I meet You face to face? Peace without end, love without limit, life without sorrow? Jesus, I love to imagine this on the day You've chosen!

1 Corinthians 2:9
However, as it is written: "What no eye has seen, what no ear has heard, and what no human mind has conceived"— the things God has prepared for those who love Him—

For other books by Judith Rolfs visit
Judith Rolfs' Amazon Author Page
And her website: www.judithrolfs.com

May *Jesus Time, Love Notes of Wonder and Worship*, her website, blog, books, articles and every speaking opportunity proclaim the wonders of our amazing, ever-loving God.

Made in the USA
Monee, IL
24 July 2023

39846350R00207